Kay.

This book is more than learning how to sell. Its about choosing, learning. and becoming all we can be.

Doug.

GOING
FOR THE
GREEN

SELLING IN THE 21ST CENTURY

By

Doug Peterson

with Walter G. Meyer

 LTI Publishing

LTI Publishing
116 Lands End Court, Suite 100
Piney Flats, Tennessee 37686

(877)244-5664 Fax (423)283-9302
ltipublishing.com
going4thegreen.com

Publisher's Cataloging-in-Publication

Peterson, Douglas K.
  Going for the green: selling in the 21st century/
  Douglas Peterson. – 1st ed.
  p. cm.
  LCCN: 00-111293
  ISBN: 0-9706909-9-1

  1. Selling   2. Marketing   3. Title

HF5438.25.P48 2001   658.85
                                   QB100-1015

Printed in the United States of America

ACKNOWLEDGEMENTS

This book is an accumulation of more than 30 years experience in sales, business and life. With a time span of so many years it goes without saying that there have been many contributors. I am certain to unwittingly leave someone out.

David McNally, author, speaker, and a friend of more than 25 years, convinced me to write this book during a round of golf at Pelican Hills in Newport Beach, California. During one of our breaks, David asked what was keeping me busy. After explaining the seminars I was facilitating on the impact of the information (digital) age on the sales function, David said, "You really ought to write a book about this. This is a major shift that will impact a lot of companies and people."

Back at the clubhouse, he asked, "Well, are you going to do it?" I agreed but with some mixed feelings about the project. David, being a little on the persistent-side, asked again, with a look of disbelief, "Will you really write it?" A little louder and with more commitment, I responded, "Yes, David. It's a done deal!" If I ever wanted to enjoy another round of golf with David, I knew I had to follow through with the commitment or he would never let me forget it. Thanks, David!

Fortunately for me, my first sales training experience was with Larry Wilson, founder of Wilson Learning. Before attending training sessions, I was "not sold" on the merit of selling as a career. My impression was that most salespeople were just one step out of prison. Larry introduced a philosophy that has stuck with me to this day: *The role of a sales person is to solve problems.* "Win-win" and "trust" were the foundations to being a successful salesperson in order to leverage long-term relationships. I embraced these concepts and am grateful for the benefits I have received over the years. Thank you Larry.

I am also grateful to the thousands of salespeople who have attended our training and development sessions over the years and who have kept me in touch with the shifts and changes occurring in their sales environment.

A special thank you to Walt Meyer, contributing writer, who worked with me to understand the issues facing sales today. I am also thankful for his flexibility when I made changes.

For the positive encouragement of my wife, Julia Losby, I am indeed grateful. She diligently read and edited many versions of the manuscript, always believing the project was exciting.

Thank you to the clients, associates, and friends, who read the manuscript and made suggestions: Robert Beauchamp and Tom Cobb of Accenture (formerly Andersen Consulting); Joe Kelly, Diagnostic Products Corp; Mike Crosby, my associate at Leadership Technologies; Jim Cadenhead of IBM; Sylvia King, Meridian West; Tom Larkin, Ronald Blue and Company; Mike Boland, Performance Technologies; David McNally, Trans-form Corporation; Mic Lucas, Wilson Learning; and finally Ruth Peterson, my mother. Your suggestions and encouragement were critical to the completion of "Going for the Green, *Selling in the 21st Century.*"

Thank you to my editor, Kellie Crowe, and designer, Myra Danehy, who eagerly jumped into this project with enthusiasm and creativity.

Finally, but not least, Kori Slagle, who took on the project to manage. Without her gentle nudging, the book would still be unfinished.

— *Douglas Peterson*

TABLE OF CONTENTS

INTRODUCTION

"Going for the Green" is a "how-to-book" written in the form of a novel. The story of Sharon and her associates is fiction. Any resemblance to actual people or companies is coincidental. The problems she, the other characters in the story, and their companies face are very real. This book is intended to serve as a guide, helping salespersons adjust to the ever-changing times ushered in by the rapid upheaval of technology. While Sharon and her counterparts are fictional, information as to how the world is changing is accurate.

The book can be used a number of different ways. It can be read simply as a novel—the story of a single mother who, suddenly about to lose her job through no fault of her own, discovers a new world of unrealized opportunity.

Or, used as a learning tool, the narrative will help explain, through example, the way the world is changing and how a salesperson who wants to succeed in this new game can adapt.

Although the specifics of Sharon's fictional case will be different, the generalities of the changes would apply to many salespersons in various fields. Before continuing to the next chapter, the reader may want to take a moment to examine his or her own problems which parallel the ones Sharon is facing, and how solutions similar to the ones Sharon discovers, can be applied.

Tables of organization for the two key fictional companies are provided at the end of the book, in **Appendix A**.

Much of the book takes place on the golf course, giving a double meaning to the title "Going for the Green." For the non-golfer, a brief guide to the **golf terminology** is given in **Appendix B**.

Appendix C provides information **about the author**.

GOING
FOR THE
GREEN

SELLING IN THE
21ST CENTURY

CHAPTER ONE

On the cliffs

Sharon Kelly stood staring in disbelief as Jeff Lee's company car pulled out of the golf course parking lot.

"Did he leave?"

Sharon turned to see Joan, who had just returned from the ladies' room, now standing behind her. Joan wiped her hands again on her golf towel.

"Yes," Sharon answered, still not sure herself if it were true. "Had to get back to the office."

"Do you have to go? Or do you still want to play the back nine?" the older woman asked.

"Why not. I've nothing else to do."

Joan looked at her quizzically.

"Fourth major account I've lost in two months," Sharon said with obvious frustration as they walked toward the 10th tee.

Joan offered a look of concern. "I hope I didn't interfere with any business you two were discussing. When I asked the starter to pair me up with someone, I made it clear that I wasn't looking to be in anyone's way."

"No, your joining us was not my problem I assure you."

"I like to meet new people," explained Joan. "I could go play with the ladies up at my club, but I like to talk about something other than who died or went to the hospital this week. Playing a public course like this, you never know who you'll come across."

"True," Sharon nodded. "Even a salesperson in a slump."

Joan smiled. "I'm one of those people who even likes to talk to a person on an airplane. Everyone has an interesting story, if you're willing to listen. But again, I certainly didn't mean to impose."

"No, not at all."

The two women played the tenth and eleventh holes in relative quiet. Sharon was engrossed in her thoughts, still believing Jeff had faked the page that prematurely ended their golf game. Only a triumvirate of F-14's screaming overhead disturbed the tranquility. Moments later a dozen crows came swooping low making a racket almost comparable to that of the jets.

"Sometimes it seems as though the crows are jealous of those jets and want to see if they can be as annoying," Joan said with a smile.

"I think the Navy is still ahead in the noise department," Sharon replied.

"Some days my money would be on the crows," Joan playfully insisted. "That is the only thing I don't like about Torrey Pines. The noise. Otherwise it would be so peaceful."

"It is beautiful out here," Sharon seconded. "The only thing that bothers me is the fear that one of these days I am really going to shank one and kill a sunbather on the beach down there." Sharon pointed toward the tight folds of the brown cliffs that dropped sharply out of view and down to the Pacific Ocean.

Sharon selected a 3-wood for the par 3, 12th hole. The clouds which had started to obscure the sun matched her darkening mood. Attempting to vent all her frustrations in one blow, she clobbered the ball and over-shot the green by a good twenty yards.

Sharon jammed the club into her bag in disgust and turned to Joan, "I guess I can't play golf anymore, either. I can't sell and I can't play golf. If this keeps up, I won't have a job or a hobby."

Joan used her 3-iron and made the shot Sharon had attempted, leaving her ball on the green about ten feet from the pin. "Are things that bad at work?"

"Well, they're not good that's for sure. Jeff, the guy we

were playing with, has bought software from me for years, but lately he's been giving me the runaround. I thought that if I could get him out for a game of golf I could get some insight into what's been going on."

As they walked toward the green, Joan had a putter in her hand, Sharon a wedge in hers. Sharon continued to talk, "I have so much of my life wrapped up in my job, and now that it's hanging by a thread, it's scary." Joan put her hand on Sharon's shoulder. "It's especially scary being a single mother. I've built a pretty secure life for my son, but if I lose my job, that would all change. I'm working harder than ever, but I'm just not getting the results I used to. I don't get it. Did you ever wake up one morning and feel you just couldn't hack it anymore?" Sharon asked as she walked down the slope to her ball.

Joan stood to the side of the green to watch. "Mind some advice?"

Sharon looked up and smiled.

Joan returned the smile. "I don't want to try to mother the world, so you can tell me to be quiet, if you want."

"No, please. Go on."

The few sage witticisms and comments Joan had dropped during the first nine holes made Sharon willing to listen.

"Golf is supposed to free your mind to think about other things—not cause more frustration. You've been using that wedge like a spade all day. Gophers do less damage. Lighten up. Relax."

"Thanks." Sharon took a deep breath but then hacked hard at the ball sending it sailing over the green, barely missing Joan. "FORE!" Sharon yelled as the ball flew past. "Sorry."

"It's okay. But if you don't want my advice, just say so," Joan joked.

"I wasn't aiming at you, honest. I am just so frustrated. These last few months have been really hard. I'm putting in more hours and bringing home less money. I can see my job slipping away. I also feel like I'm neglecting my son. Then I come out here and make a botch of this as well."

"Are you botching the job?"

Sharon paused between her short shots to look at Joan as she started to wonder who this woman was and why she appeared so interested in her. The older woman smiled and said, "Jeff told me you've been business associates for years, and that he likes doing business with you because you're so good at what you do. He also said you provide great service. Maybe you need to get your people to lower the price or improve the product. Or, go to work selling for your competitor."

"I'm not sure, that's the answer," Sharon said as she watched Joan hit first a long putt and then a short one for her own par. "The differences in our products and those of our competitors are so small, that if one company makes a change, the others just copy it or do something close within three or four months. If it becomes just a price war, then we all lose. And there's no stability even in switching companies, if next week someone else undercuts the entire industry. You see this in so many industries—a big company spends a fortune on R & D; some little start-up company reverse engineers it...."

Joan's brow furrowed in confusion.

"That is, takes it apart to see how it works," Sharon clarified, "and makes a knock-off in a month, sometimes less. It used to be if you invested the time and energy to develop a new product, you had time to make a profit from it before all the imitators entered the field. There are people writing software in their dens that can almost compete with the big boys these days. A company like mine has so much bureaucracy, they have to charge more. The competition is simply eating us alive."

They walked to the 13th and sat on the bench while waiting for the foursome in front of them to clear the fairway.

"Are you worried more about the competition, or what

you're doing?" Joan asked.

As if she didn't hear the question Sharon sighed, "Maybe I should give up sales."

"Or give up selling the product," Joan said cryptically. "It sounds like you have hit the wall."

"The wall?"

"One of my sons-in-law runs marathons—"

"Oh yes. I am *quite* familiar with that term. Somewhere around the 15-to-20 mile mark, usually, people run out of energy. Your body sort of gives up."

"You run marathons?" Joan raised her eyebrows, impressed.

"One. Years ago. Right after college. Never again." Sharon smiled as though even the memory wore her out.

"What was your time?"

"About four days, I think."

"But you finished?"

"Oh yes, I finished."

"So you ran past the wall? I think you've hit a similar barrier now. But this time it's a wall of complexity."

"Wall of complexity?"

"Things appear too complicated right now. We've all been there—in relationships, jobs, all sorts of situations. And you have to decide if the relationship, job—whatever—is worth saving. And if so, you need to sort through this tornado of confusing issues and tackle them one at time."

Sharon nodded. "My sister called me last night, in tears. She's planning her wedding and the 'to-do list' got to her."

Joan shook her head. "Been there, done that. Four weddings, in fact! Two of my own and two of my daughters. It's pretty daunting, unless you take it step by step. Your sister hit the wall last night. She let THE WEDDING, one of the most important events in her life, scare her to the point she couldn't think straight. But, if you take it as little things which anyone can do—call the caterer, call the florist. Each one at a time. It's a piece of cake. A lot of work, but a piece of cake. Wedding cake, to be exact," Joan quipped. "It's the same thing now. You're letting the problem overwhelm you."

Joan then swung her driver with an ease that seemed to belie her age.

Sharon's ultra-tense swing, in contrast, produced a drive that looked like an errant Scud Missile as it went screaming into the trees.

Staring at the wooded area that had swallowed Sharon's ball to such a depth that a search party would be unlikely to find it, Joan continued, "I think that last shot just proves the old adage: *Don't think and drive.*"

Sharon smiled and exhaled half a laugh. "I guess you're right. With your permission I'll just play a provisional ball and forget that one."

Even though all Sharon could think about was work and her future, she forced herself to try to get off the subject for a little while as they walked along the edge of the fairway, the cliffs offering their scenic view to the left. "It almost looks like it might rain," she said, pointing to the darkening clouds.

"I doubt it," Joan said. "Not the right kind of clouds. Besides, I prefer the notion of it being partially sunny rather than partially cloudy. It gives me more hope."

Sharon pointed with her club toward where a rabbit chewed on some grass. It crinkled its nose as the women approached, but did not move.

"See, bunnies aren't dumb," commented Joan. "*Dumb bunny* is just a saying. If it were going to rain, the bunny would have taken cover by now. He's not expecting the worst, but he is prepared for it. I'm sure that little fella isn't far from his hole. And, like the bunny, I'm always prepared," Joan said, using her club to tap the golf umbrella on the side of her bag. "Plan for the best, but prepare for the worst."

"Sounds like a good philosophy," Sharon said as she began to feel not only intrigued by what her new acquaintance was saying but somehow also comforted.

Joan smiled and said, "I love the spring. The fresh smell, the flowers, the baby bunnies." She pointed to where several smaller rabbits were eating. "I planned my vacation early this year so I could come back in time to welcome the season."

Joan took a deep breath to enjoy the scent as the sun baked the moisture from the fairway. Sharon noticed that Joan did seem rather tan for this early in the year. "Where did you go on vacation?" she asked.

"Aruba."

"Sounds nice."

"It was lovely. I went with my friend Ruth. She is a widow, too. It was funny. We told our friend Agnes we were going to Aruba, and Agnes said, 'Aruba, where's that?' and Ruth said, 'I don't know. Joan made the reservations. Besides, what difference does it make? We're flying.'"

Sharon laughed. Her first good laugh in a week she realized. Even the comedy she had rented and watched with her son, Max, the night before had failed to amuse her. When Sharon stopped laughing she said, "Good point. As long as you're not the one driving or navigating, it doesn't matter where it is."

Joan watched in silence as Sharon muffed the fairway shot. "It looks like you could use a vacation."

"I really could. But it could be an involuntary vacation if things don't improve."

After watching Sharon four-putt, the older woman asked with concern, "This is really eating you up, isn't it?"

Sharon nodded. "I just can't shake the idea," she said as she returned the putter to her bag, "that I'm the problem. Jeff and my other clients always liked me enough that even if they could get the same for a little less elsewhere, they stayed with me."

Joan nodded and played her shot. They played most of the next hole chatting about Aruba.

Until these ramblings about her elderly friends, Joan had not struck Sharon as old at all. Now that Sharon tried to assess it, she wasn't sure if Joan were an old sixty-year-old or—more likely, Sharon thought—she is probably a very youthful septuagenarian. Joan seemed in perfect physical health and swung her club with as much authority and speed as Sharon. She seemed very intelligent, was very well dressed, and used a set of clubs that Sharon knew set someone back a few thousand dollars. They were the kind that Sharon could never justify buying—not with a twelve-year-old to dress in clothes he seemed to outgrow daily, and who would probably not only want to go to college, but insist on eating in the meantime.

Although Joan maintained honors on the next hole, she told Sharon to go ahead and hit her drive while she re-laced a shoe. Sharon's drive once again failed to curve back and went sailing into the woods ricocheting through the newly green trees. Sharon turned to Joan and shook her head.

Joan looked to see that the foursome behind them was not even near the last green. Joan smiled and then asked tentatively, "Want a tad more advice?"

Sharon smiled. "After a shot like that, it couldn't hurt."

"No, it couldn't," Joan agreed. Joan passed on some advice about repositioning her feet that a pro had given her when she had taken her annual pre-season lesson.

When she was finished, Sharon protested, "But I've always lined up my feet with the flag."

Joan looked off at the trees, and then said with polite sarcasm, "And has it always worked this well?"

Sharon let out a laugh.

"If what you've always done doesn't work any more," Joan continued, "then what have you got to lose by trying something different?"

Sharon opened her mouth to speak, but Joan interrupted her, "Don't say *a ball*. You just did that."

"Good point," Sharon conceded, laughing again.

10

Joan approached the ball and took her shot. It followed Sharon's into the trees. Joan winced as though she could feel the ball's pain as it snapped twigs on its flight.

As Joan slid her driver back into her bag, she turned to Sharon, smiled and said, "Golf course leprechauns."

Sharon stared at Joan bemused.

"Course leprechauns," Joan repeated before Sharon could even form the question on her lips. "Surely you've heard all the jokes about golfers finding leprechauns in the woods around golf courses. I blame my bad shots on the evil ones. I can't get all worked up about it if I miss-hit a shot. Everything that happens to you in life is *not* your fault. Sometimes you do everything you can, and due to circumstances completely beyond your control, things don't go the way they were supposed to. It happens and I can't second guess or beat myself up over it when it does. It's as good an explanation as any and it keeps me from going crazy when I shank one now and then."

Sharon looked puzzled.

"Don't look at me like that," said Joan. "I don't really believe in leprechauns. It just gets me past my bad shots."

"I didn't think you did. But you just told me—"

Joan smiled and held up her gloved hand to silence Sharon. "That was my first really bad drive of the day, wouldn't you say?"

Sharon nodded in agreement.

"So rather than worry about it and get so tensed that I over-analyze my swing to the point that I can't hit anything, I prefer to forget about it. I like to blame it on something crazy over which I have no control, then I can relax and enjoy golf."

Sharon opened her mouth as if to question but Joan went on, "But, if everything you hit is going off in the same wrong direction, then it's time to make a correction."

Sharon nodded and the ladies each hit new, somewhat better drives. As they walked from the tee, Joan patted Sharon's shoulder. "Don't let this make you crazy. Even when you have to make corrections, just accept that things aren't working and it's time to try something else. Don't be too hard on yourself. You get so tense you can't hit because you're thinking too much. It's no way to have fun on the golf course—or in life for that matter. I've seen several friends have their golf game destroyed by the fear that they could no longer play well and this eroding confidence whittled away at their skills even more." Sharon studied Joan again and wondered if she were still talking about golf. "But there are times when you have to ask yourself what you can do differently to change your game. Where can you find the new advantage? What bit of information can change the whole way you look at things? The difference between a good golfer and a great one is only one or two strokes per round."

They walked toward the trees, each with a ball in her hands, and Joan continued talking, "People don't like to change. Events make us change. My son was transferred to Spain. His wife and kids didn't want to go—went dragging their feet as a matter of fact. After two years there they found they liked it so much that when his contract was up and it was time to come back, they wanted to stay. We make changes so reluctantly, but if we are ever forced to change, we may actually find that the change we resisted was for the better."

The women played their next shots from the fairway, not far from where their balls had disappeared out of bounds, beyond the signs that warned of snakes on the cliffs. As they walked toward the green, Joan resumed the lesson. "On any shot how many things can happen?"

Sharon frowned. "It could go in the trees, in the water, in the sand...."

Joan shook her head to stop the recitation. "Too negative. Only two things can happen: It will go in the hole or it won't. Once you take a moment to realize you can handle the joy if it does go in or the mild disappointment if it doesn't, and that the match does not hang on this one shot either way, you can relax.

You don't have to fear every shot. If successful, give yourself an *'attagirl'* and move on to the next hole. If not, you try again. Either way, it's not the end of the world."

After they finished up eighteen, Joan suggested they hit the snack bar for an iced tea. And Sharon, after first checking her watch to make sure she would still be home before her son, accepted.

As they walked, their soft golf cleats squeaked on the asphalt path.

"One thing that frustrates golfers is they want to compare every shot to the best one they ever made, so they feel like they are failing 99 percent of the time," Joan said.

"Salespeople do the same thing. They compare every sale to that one dream sale where you walk in and they buy everything before you even open your mouth."

"You have to be realistic. Not every shot or every sale is going to go perfectly. You have to enjoy it when it does, but know most will take a little more effort than that." Continuing their conversational banter comparing golf and work, Joan zeroed in on Sharon's current situation. "So your software is not doing what they want it to?"

"I guess not. The new version *was* due out this year—had some glitches—and now many of my customers are looking elsewhere. It could be six months, or even a year, before our tech people straighten things out. I'm just afraid the cost—which is already a little higher than the industry average—will have to be even higher to pay for these delays. It used to be that my customers stuck with me even during times like this. No one has loyalty anymore."

"Bah," Joan scoffed. "Loyalty is what salespeople call it when customers continue buying from them over a period of time. Loyalty is what the salesman said my father had when he continued buying Fords while they were selling Chevys down the block for two hundred dollars less."

Sharon looked at Joan. The older woman continued, "Back

on the fifth hole, why didn't you use a driver for your second shot?"

"A driver? That's what I used off the tee—I would have killed somebody on the beach. I almost overshot the green with a 9-iron."

"So you wanted the best tool for the job? Not the one that was already in hand?" Joan shook her head in mock disapproval. "It served you well on the last shot, but you had no loyalty to it!"

Sharon smiled, "Point taken."

"I'd say the 9-iron was the right choice. You made the green."

"And you didn't," Sharon smiled.

"But then you can't always blame the club either," she grinned back.

"Leprechauns?" Sharon offered.

"Must have been. So is yours the only company whose sales are suffering?"

"No, far from it. The industry is changing. Everyone's getting hit hard. We've had to let a few people go. Our two main competitors, LatCo and Reese, have too."

"Just too much competition?"

"Yep, too many new little players in the game changing the whole setup."

"How do your clients use your software?"

Sharon looked puzzled.

Joan continued, "That nice young man we played the front nine with, Jeff, did you ever ask him what his company's goals are this year and how does his job help in achieving those goals? Or how he is being measured?"

Sharon let the questions sink in.

"Maybe you became too comfortable with your approach," Joan gently suggested. "You may have thought that Jeff would automatically give you the business, due to the excellent service and relationship you've developed over the years, so you didn't have to re-sell him, or his company, on your value."

Sharon thought for a moment before answering. "You may be right. Without realizing it, I may have dismissed the most basic rule of selling: You have to keep re-earning the customer's business everyday."

"Don't be too hard on yourself. We all get complacent at times."

"Honestly, I knew everything I needed to make the sale with him for ten years. I knew the software and its applications. I know the size of Jeff's department, and what functions it performs."

"But obviously, that's not enough anymore. Perhaps you need to get a sense of the big picture," Joan said.

For a moment, Sharon wondered if Joan was questioning whether she knew how to do her job. Sharon had kept Jeff's business for ten years. That proved something.

"Have you played this course before?" Joan asked, suddenly getting back to golf, or so Sharon thought.

"Yes. Many times."

"So you know the 3rd hole?"

"The dogleg."

"That's the one. Do you try to hit your second shot long, to that nice open space to the left of the bunker?"

"Assuming the way that I am hitting them and that my shot may actually go where I wanted it to—no."

"Why not?"

"Because there is no way to make the angle to the green."

"So you're better off playing it short of the bunker?"

"That's what I aim for. It doesn't always go there, but that's what I aim for."

"So what seems like the way to do it—hit away to that nice open stretch of fairway—is not necessarily the best way," Joan concluded. "I made the *go long to the left* mistake myself a few times before I learned. I realized a different approach would work better when you go for the green."

Sharon let this digest. After their iced teas arrived, she asked, "Are you in the business also?"

"Oh, not really. Not any more at least," Joan laughed. "I just play—golf, tennis, bridge—and do a little volunteer work."

"Sounds like you keep busy."

"I try. Work hard. Play hard. Give back more than you take. That has always been my philosophy."

Sharon smiled appreciatively. "Good philosophy."

"And I've found that if I do the *right* work well, whether volunteer or paid, it does not seem much like work, but becomes fun as well. I have known too many people who died young without ever enjoying life. They saw work and fun as two different things. I try to have fun with whatever I do, so I don't go to my grave regretting all that time spent doing things I hated or should not have been doing."

Sharon sipped her iced tea and nodded appreciatively.

"I've found that in most other areas of my life, if things got too difficult, it was because I was doing something wrong. If every day was a constant struggle, it usually meant I was going in the wrong direction. When I found the right path, things got easier. Not necessarily easy—there were still obstacles, problems, and challenges—but not every movement seemed a major effort made twice as difficult because it appeared destined for failure. Reminds me of the joke about the man who buys a chain saw...." Joan paused to see if Sharon had heard it.

Sharon shook her head and then nodded for Joan to continue.

"Man buys a chain saw. Sees the sign in the hardware store that says it cuts ten cords of wood a day. So he buys it, takes it home. The next day he works with it all day and only cuts half a cord. So he assumes he must be doing something wrong. The next day he gets up earlier, and works later, with no breaks all day, but still only manages to cut one cord. So he takes it back to the hardware store and tells the clerk there must be

16

something wrong with it. The clerk says, 'Let's see,' and pulls the starter cord. The chain saw roars to life—RRRRRRRR—and the man says, 'What's that noise?'"

Sharon laughed. "Very funny. And I especially like the chain saw imitation."

Joan also laughed, then added, "But it seems to me you need to find a way to re-start your chain saw. If things have gotten that hard, something needs to be corrected. Look into how you can help Jeff do his job easier, and it just may make your job easier."

"On the cliffs"

As a salesperson, have you "hit the wall" in your competitive selling environment?

- Are you losing "loyal customers" to competitors who are selling good products at lower prices?
- Is your product and service viewed by customers as commodity-like?
- Does it seem as though you require new "leading-edge" products to win and keep customers?

Traditionally, salespeople have counted on having the best product, a good relationship, or the lowest price in order to win business. In this selling environment, salespeople, like Sharon, have been able to achieve excellent performance by exercising their interpersonal, service and technical skills.

Yet, in today's hyper-competitive environment, salespeople need a new source of advantage in order to win. Sharon is "on the cliff" of her career where she will have to change her approach in order to win and keep customers.

Sharon, like many other salespeople in almost every industry today, needs a "new source of advantage"— something that will cause her and her product to stand out from all of the rest.

CHAPTER TWO

Studying the links

Sharon drove home from Torrey Pines with her head buzzing. Not since her first sales call—could it really have been fourteen years earlier—had she felt so unsure and incompetent. After that first call, she had lingered in her car in the parking lot, pretending to get her things together. In reality she was stalling for it to be time for the man with whom she had had her appointment to leave. She hoped to just sort of "run into" him in the parking lot in hopes of redeeming the botch she had made of the pitch. It didn't work. Her last-ditch effort in the parking lot had not saved it, and she came away empty-handed and dejected.

At the time it seemed as though her world would end if she did not get the order, but it did not. She somehow mustered the courage to go back and face the dragon again the next day, and again the day after that. It was a week before she actually made a sale, but she was learning from her mistakes. And, now she was realizing that it was once again time to go back to the school of hard knocks. There were more lessons to be learned.

All the things she had learned in those first few weeks and months at Scarleton selling office supplies had served her well as she progressed from what now seemed like a small operation to her current sales job. She eventually quit Scarleton to have her son. She then started first part-time, and later full-time, at Software Solutions, Inc., where she had now worked for almost ten years at selling software to industrial manufacturers.

Now, much more was at stake. If she did not find a way to make her job work again, she would be unemployed in a few months. Things were too tight these days at SSI for them to carry dead wood for very long. As Software Solution's sales-*man* of the year for five of the past seven years, she was the one for whom they had to change the plaque to read "Sales*person* of the year." It was hard for her to start thinking of herself as one of those marginal performers who barely made the cut, quarter after quarter. Sharon knew she was still good, but felt like some of those PGA players, who, although they are still in the top twenty money-winners, are considered has-beens because they have not won a major in ten years.

Sharon wondered if her sales slump had already driven her crazy. She felt like conceding the quarter, and she was never a quitter; only there seemed so little reason to hope that things would be any better next quarter, either. Sharon had not made a single successful sales call all week. Even her call on E.F. Striepeke & Co. had gone badly. Yet, sadly enough, even if they had bought, their purchase order would have been so small, it wouldn't made a dent in her quota for the quarter.

If things did not turn around at work, Sharon knew she would have to give up golf. It was a time and money con-suming luxury. Actually, she was often undecided as to whether golf was a perk she gave herself or a justifiable expen-diture of business time and money. To a large degree, she cred-ited golf with helping her make it to the big time in sales. She noticed that all the top performers at Scarleton played golf. They networked on the course and at their clubs. There was a 'good ol' boy' clique at Scarleton, and she realized to get the leads she wanted, it would be necessary to fit in.

Growing up, watching her father tiptoe out of the house at some ridiculously early hour every Saturday to chase a white ball with a stick, seemed to Sharon to be a particularly ludicrous pursuit. However, when she realized what an asset it could be to her career, she struck out for the course — and struck out on the course. Rather than scoring points with the guys, she was holding up play, and annoying her fellow salespeople, not to mention whatever foursome had the misfortune to follow her.

Like everything else Sharon had ever done, however, she resolved if she was going to do it, she was going to do it well. When pointers from her father failed to make her a competent golfer, she took lessons from a pro until she could swing a club with authority. Sharon always believed in learning more about a subject from those who knew it best. With proper guidance, she worked on her game until, given the advantage of the red tees, she could hold her own with the best of the average amateurs with whom she played. The sales division's golf gurus now sometimes asked her to play when ego was on the line in some of the friendly interdepartmental or inter-company rivalries that popped up now and then. Sharon attributed some of her most solid business relationships, like the one with Jeff Lee, to time spent with them on the links. Sometimes Jeff's wife, Jackie, would join them for a round. Now, Sharon was watching her golf game, like her sales skills, slip away.

She saw her friend Craig as sort of the 'ghost of Christmas future.' He never made his quota three of four quarters last year. It was quit or be fired. After months of searching, he finally found a 42K-a-year job in computer services for an insurance company. He hated it. He lamented giving up the freedom to set your own hours and being out on the road, to being cooped up in an office. And he found it even tougher to take a cut from close to six-figures, which is where he was, to less than half that. His wife, Suzy, had to go back to work. Sharon knew Suzy planned to eventually, but not full-time, and then not until their youngest was in first grade. At least they had that option. As a single parent, Sharon didn't have the option of a second income without a second job. She saw her son little enough as it was. She shuddered when she thought about what a hit their lifestyle would take if she lost her job.

As long as she was making good money, she could afford luxuries like a part-time housekeeper. Someone to help with the cleaning gave her more time and energy for her son. And, she used golf as her one form of recreation—as well as for business. That would end if she lost her job.

She felt like a range ball on a Saturday night—beaten and hacked at all week. She had only sold 40 percent of what she was expected to sell this quarter and had budgeted the sale to Jeff to be most of that. She had already spent her draw, and was counting on the quarterly bonus to pay the big bills.

She was so lost in thought that pulling into her own driveway, still on auto-pilot, startled her.

That evening, after dinner, Sharon sat in front of the computer exasperated. An hour and a half of searching the web had brought her articles in German, French, and what she assumed to be Russian. She had found information on ice-age tools in Norway, sheep-shearing tools in Australia, and Peter O'Toole. What she had not found was any information about Jeff's company, ToolTech.

How could this be? Did she really know this little about surfing the web? She was not computer illiterate—far from it—she sold sophisticated software! She heard people talking all the time about *searching the web*, but could not believe this was the first time she had ever tried to find something that she really HAD to find and that it was so difficult. She had always been too busy with work to do more than play around a little, cyber-surfing for fun. Joan had managed to do everything from booking a trip to Aruba to finding their family tree on-line. How did she do it?

Sharon had no trouble finding web sites when she knew an address, and she had ordered things and shopped on-line, but random searching like this seemed a pointless endeavor, unless there was a trick to it she did not know.

Some words she entered brought back more than a million matches, and that was as bad as none since she could not begin to check them all out. Surfing for fun was one thing—but she was in dire need of *answers*. Her frustration was such that she was on the verge of road rage on the information superhighway.

Maybe it was true, as Joan had theorized, that everyone born since 1969 had a chip implanted in their brain that made everything about computers instantly comprehensible. Those born before the moon landing were doomed to forever hit ENTER repeatedly while cursing under their breath.

Sharon stared at the computer screen, lost in thought.

Her late afternoon phone call to Jeff Lee had yielded almost no more information about ToolTech beyond what she already knew. Other than a few vague generalities of the type she had handed Joan, Jeff Lee seemed to know so little about his own company. He had worked for ToolTech for twenty years and yet seemed pretty much unaware of what his company was up to, and could only name a few of its major customers. Jeff pointed out that he had nothing to do with the bottom line, or the finished product. He just did purchasing for one little division. Sure he knew what they made, but Sharon was surprised to learn he did not really seem too terribly interested in what companies bought ToolTech's machinery, or what they did with it.

He had been able to do purchasing for twenty years without having to know, so why worry about it now? She didn't press him harder, because she felt strange trying to explain to him why she wanted the information since, as they both acknowledged, she had already lost the account. She could also sense that Jeff did not completely buy her explanation that it was for a win/loss report she was doing. The reports were standard with some companies, but never with questions that probed far beyond just the product and the buyer's department. She was sure Jeff knew more, but she didn't know how to pick his brain any further without making them both uncomfortable.

When the screen saver started rotating the planets in space, she realized she had been staring at the screen for too long without doing anything. She was about to click 'shut down' on the computer when she felt hands on her shoulders.

"Hey, Mom, whatcha doing?"

"Giving up," she replied. Even as she said it, it struck her that not so long ago, that phrase was not a part of her vocabulary.

"On what?"

"Did you get your homework done?"

"Yep," Sharon's twelve-year-old, Max, replied as he leaned over her shoulder to look at the computer screen. "You're looking up stuff about Peter O'Toole? Who's he?"

"An actor. And I'm not. I'm lost in cyberspace. I was looking up something else and I got stuck here."

"You weren't trying to look this up?"

"No, but I can't get it to find what I want."

"It's no wonder. The search engine you're using is the pits."

"It's the one that came on when I got on-line."

"Yeah, that's 'cause they like pay to be there. That's the only reason anybody would use that lame thing. You need a decent one. Type in W-W-W-dot— Here."

He reached around her and typed in a web address.

*   *   *   *   *   *   *   *   *

Two hours later, a bleary-eyed Sharon rubbed her face.

"Max, I think it's past your bed time."

"You don't need any more help?"

"I do, but you need your sleep. And you've found me plenty to read already."

As proof, she held up a stack of articles and reports they had printed off the web. That stack was in addition to longer, more involved things, such as ToolTech's annual report, which they had bookmarked on the computer. She switched screens and counted. There were seventeen other sites bookmarked and waiting for her to explore. Many, she recalled, also had links to

24

many other sites worth investigating.

"Max, my boy, you are amazing. I could never have found all of this."

"It's no big deal," he shrugged.

"All of those nights you were glued to this thing, I thought you were playing that goofy Starship Warrior thing."

"I do that, too," he smiled. "But at school, we get assignments to look up stuff on the web. So I just found the best search engine and let it do the work for me."

"Well, I'm impressed. You're a big help. Thank you."

She hugged her son and although he did the embarrassed push-away, she saw the look of pride and accomplishment on his face. It was one of those bonding moments that was even more precious to Sharon since they seemed to be getting more rare lately.

"Sorry to monopolize the computer all night," she said to break the tension before she started to cry.

"No problem. Got any more questions, ask. It was kind of fun to look up real stuff instead of just some lame assignment for school."

She looked at him and could have sworn he had grown since yesterday.

*   *   *   *   *   *   *   *   *

Sharon yawned as she rinsed the dishes and put them in the dishwasher. She couldn't believe she had stayed up until four in the morning surfing the web, following the links which Max had found for her. She had heard about web addicts and now she understood how that was possible.

She remembered a few years ago her neighbor saying he has stayed up all night watching live, real-time trading of sheep futures in Australia. When she asked him why, he said,

"Because I can!" The information available on the web was so vast and detailed, that Sharon had fought hard to stay focused on the task at hand, and not follow every link that sounded interesting. A couple times she had taken those detours and found herself reading about tennis instead of business and wondered how she had come to be on a sports site. She would trace back the links, like a trail of bread crumbs, to see that some employee, somewhere, while doing the company site, had included a few of his or her favorite sites among the links to other places of interest to business readers.

Other than a few perfunctory phone calls, she had spent the better part of the day reading what he had printed for her last night. She could not believe Max had found so much information after her hour and a half search had yielded nothing. It just proved the same lesson she applied in other areas of her life: If you want to know something, ask an expert, even if he is twelve years old.

She wondered how to justify this major expenditure of time. In the old days of logging sales calls and results, this kind of 'research' had no place and would have been seen by most managers as a waste of time. She was still pretty sure that if she told her boss, Alan, how she had spent her day, he would have seen it as pointless.

Sharon actually enjoyed the small domestic tasks like doing the dishes. She missed doing simple things and worried she was becoming a workaholic. She found herself spending more and more time to make fewer dollars. She had been so busy lately, that she had not done anything to make her feel at home in a while. She had also neglected many of her friends, and wondered if that was why she had found the time with Joan so enjoyable. It was a good thing that Joan was so patient, because most of Sharon's friends had such full schedules themselves that they would not have had time to listen to Sharon's woes.

Sharon liked doing small chores like this for the same reason her father had once admitted he liked cutting the grass. She had offered to help, and he had declined. He always said "mowing keeps your hands busy to free your mind to think about other things." If you just wandered around the backyard or stood in the kitchen doing nothing, people would think you were weird. But if you are doing an important chore, people will leave you alone, and you can think. You scored points for doing a much-needed task, and everyone left you alone for fear of being asked to help. Her father once asserted that if more people had lawn mowers we would need fewer psychiatrists.

It was not that Max never helped with kitchen chores, or that Sharon did not enjoy her son's company, but right now she was enjoying a few quiet moments for herself. Sharon yawned again as she put the plate in the dishwasher, closed it and turned it on.

She walked into the family room. That name for this room always seemed to her to be too large considering it was just the two of them in this family. She expected to find Max watching television or exploring alien worlds on the computer in his favorite game, since it was Friday and he did not have to do homework.

Instead, she found him surrounded by printed pages, and the computer showed a page from *Standard and Poors*. He looked up when she entered.

"Hey, Mom, check this out. ToolTech is buying CTC."

"What?" she said, having heard him, but unable to believe she had heard right for two reasons: one, that her son sounded genuinely excited that he had stumbled across that fascinating piece of information; and two, that ToolTech, a giant in its industry, was merging. She had read a lot about ToolTech in the past twenty-four hours, but had seen nothing about this.

Max handed her a printout of an article.

"How—," Sharon started to stammer.

"I figured I'd follow a few of the links you hadn't—the ones we bookmarked, but had not changed color 'cause you hadn't clicked on them yet. Then I tried a couple different searches. Here's what I found."

He pointed to the stack of papers he had handed her. On top was a list of all of ToolTech's warehouses and offices throughout the U.S. It gave phone numbers, real estate holdings, and more. Before Sharon could even begin to digest the information, with a few keystrokes, Max brought up another article on the screen.

"It seems like ToolTech is going to buy CTC for a lot of money. I mean a lot, like more than Tiger Woods makes. And so that instead of..."

Max changed computer screens again with the flip of the mouse and brought up a chart of industrial toolmakers.

"...ToolTech being number two and CTC number four," Max continued as he flipped to another chart, "together they will be number one." Max paused. "I wasn't sure what you were looking for. Is this the kind of stuff you wanted to know?"

"Yes, please. Go on."

Sharon thought to herself; she still was not sure what she wanted to know, but like Max, she was intrigued. CTC had been a strong niche player, in an area where ToolTech was weak. Together they could dominate the industry.

Max continued, "ToolTech and CTC are both saying it's not for sure, and just preliminary negotiations."

He leafed through the papers she was holding and pointed to one.

"But everybody else thinks that is just to keep the stock price from jumping. Kind of like that hotel chain-buying game we play. I used to think the *Wall Street Journal* was boring when you would leave it around—no sports, no comics, but this is kind of cool—like a real version of our game. There's an article on-line...."

Another mouse click.

"It's from the Wall Street Journal. They didn't want it to get

28

around that there will be lots of lay-offs. Mainly in management and HR. I am not sure what that is, but I doubt it is home runs," Max joked.

Sharon smiled. "Human Resources. The people who do the hiring and firing."

Max turned from the computer to face his mother. "All of this doesn't affect you, right? I mean, you still work for SSI, right? I mean you aren't going to get fired, are you?"

"Oh, no, of course not." Sharon put a reassuring hand on Max's shoulder. She hoped he did not hear the fear she hid in her voice as she told him what she hoped was the truth.

After Max went to bed, she returned to the computer to further explore the information Max had found. There were links that connected ToolTech and its soon-to-be-acquisition, CTC, with many of their major suppliers, as well as many of their key customers. They had found articles on-line from *Barron's*, *The Wall Street Journal*, *Business Week*, and a host of other business publications. There was information in stock-buying guides on-line, and listings of industrial tool manufacturers. They had found more than 300 web sites that mentioned ToolTech or CTC. She was amazed at the host of information available to her without having to leave her family room.

Some divisions and departments of both companies even had their own web sites offering an amazing amount of insight into the companies, their organizations, people, and priorities. She was shocked she did not have a clue as to how much data was available at her fingertips, and now wondered if there were sites like these for every client with whom she did business.

Max had even found her a history of ToolTech. She learned that ToolTech was founded in 1924 by Elton Spahr as a manufacturer of farm equipment. Spahr found he could not find a machine to efficiently make the kinds of quality farm tools that he hoped to manufacture, so he started designing and making his own machines. He was a creative man who liked to tinker.

During World War II, under a government contract, the

company expanded to make items needed by the armed forces, such as entrenching tools and tent poles. After the war, the government no longer needed military equipment, and Spahr wanted to start concentrating on what he saw as ToolTech's real strength—the design and manufacture of machines to make specialty tools. He wanted to make the machines that made things, and get out of the tool business entirely. In early 1946, just as he was beginning to make the switch, the long hours and overwork caught up with Elton Spahr and he suffered a fatal heart attack.

After Spahr's death, his son-in-law, Brian Phillips, took over as the president of ToolTech. Phillips had been a sales manager for the company, and had married Elton Spahr's daughter. Spahr's daughter was the only one of his children to believe the company was salvageable, and both of her brothers had chosen other careers. Now at the helm, Phillips knew how successful he and his sales team had been selling farm tools before the war, therefore he wanted to return to that business.

For the first time in its history, ToolTech started losing money. Phillips' wife, who had inherited the company from her father, identified the problem: farming had changed. When the men who had fought the war came home to their farms, they were not going to be content to do things the old way. Many men were not going back to the farms at all, so those who did were going to need bigger and better ways of doing things to replace the diminished manpower.

Phillips would not face the reality that the company could not go backwards. He tried to insist that what had worked once *had to work again*. Spahr's daughter ended up having to use her clout as the largest shareholder of ToolTech to depose him as president. She took over the company and launched it in the direction her father had intended, and built it into the second largest manufacturer of industrial tool making machinery. Sharon was impressed that, at a time when women were rarely allowed in boardrooms, let alone at the head of the table, Spahr's daughter eventually became chair of the board of ToolTech.

The fight for the company broke up her marriage to Phillips, and she eventually married a doctor by the name of Moore, with whom she had three children. Dr. Moore was killed in a car accident in 1957, and Mrs. Moore went on doing double duty as a single mom and head of ToolTech until her retirement in 1990. Sharon found the story of this woman an inspiring one, especially in this, her own time of crisis.

Studying the links

**Do you understand your customer as a business?
Do you know how to access pertinent information about
your customer's business activities?**

1. **Annual Report:** Created annually by the client's executive team, this document includes the following: letters to shareholders, income statement, balance sheet, management discussion and analysis, stock-related information, other issues affecting the company, and key executive information.

2. **10 K Report:** This report is required by the Securities and Exchange Commission (SEC) of all publicly traded companies. The 10K report is more comprehensive than the annual report.

3. **10 Q Report:** This report is a quarterly version of the 10K and is also required by the SEC.

4. **8 Q Report:** These are official reports that inform shareholders about any major changes that may affect the company, such as a new president, acquisitions, mergers, as well as other information.

5. **Proxy Reports:** These reports are generated when a company issues stock to raise money publicly.

6. **News Releases:** These are usually generated internally by the communications department and are designed to put a positive spin on the company's potential.

7. **Client Contacts:** Individuals you interface with in the customer organization oftentimes have inside information that doesn't get published.

Sharon needs to understand the business priorities facing her client before she can craft a business solution that will have a compelling financial impact on her customer's bottom line.

Just as Sharon discovered, the Internet is an incredibly efficient research tool. Most companies today have their own web sites, where you can visit and gather most of the financial information you need. Additionally, web sites such as OneSource, Hoovers, and KnowX are great comprehensive sources of public information.

News releases can be obtained by creating a "search engine" of key words that would include your client's name. These searches will notify you when something appears in major business magazines, newspapers, and industry newsletters.

Connecting all these sources of information can give the salesperson a big picture view of the client, their industry, and their competitors. Armed with this information, salespeople can craft and position solutions that align with the company's business priorities.

Most salespeople today focus on their own products, and technology. In order for salespeople to gain a competitive advantage today they must create solutions that impact the client's business performance. This is a *market-in* approach rather than a *factory-out* approach.

CHAPTER THREE

Playing out of the rough

Sharon couldn't believe how excited she was to have so much to report back to Joan. She was glad they had scheduled a golf game for what she was already beginning to think of as their "usual" one o'clock Thursday.

Perhaps it was Joan's cool, intelligent, almost professorial air that made Sharon feel like a school girl, again—about to turn in an 'A' paper to a favorite teacher. She was sure she had done her homework well and had earned a good grade.

Sharon looked up excitedly when Joan wheeled her cart next to Sharon's in the starter's area of the South Course. After the pleasant greetings, Joan motioned to the darkening clouds out over the ocean. As they waited to tee off, hoping the storm would stay off shore, Joan asked, "So, how was your week?"

"Much better," Sharon replied with a smile.

"You made some sales this week?" Joan asked.

"No, not a one," Sharon answered, surprising herself that she could possibly be smiling about that.

"So, what made it so good, then?"

Sharon recounted how she had spent some wonderful "learning" time with Max, getting to see her son in a whole different light. "Just yesterday, it seemed he was playing with toy trucks, and now he seems to be getting ready for college!" Sharon then told Joan some of what she had learned about Jeff's company.

"The joining of these two big companies is going to shake things up quite a bit," she concluded eagerly.

"And is that a good thing or a bad thing for you?" Joan asked.

Sharon paused. Strangely, she thought, she had been so excited about the volumes of information she and Max had found, that she had not really thought about what it meant for her. Like learning the average rainfall of the Amazon basin, or the chief export of Peru, or so many other things she had learned in school, she was left with the feeling of, *'Now that I know that, what am I supposed to do with it?'* She reluctantly answered, "I don't know."

"It sounds like this could be a golden opportunity for you. There are bound to be changes and you could become part of them." Sharon contemplated that statement. Joan went on, "How will this acquisition make your client do things differently?"

Sharon was really surprised she had not asked herself Joan's question. To avoid answering it, Sharon changed the subject a bit. "I was really surprised by how little Jeff knew about his own company. I've been selling to him for more than ten years, and he seemed to know all the answers before. And, if he didn't know them, he was interested enough in the questions to want to find out. It may sound strange, but I was actually a little disappointed in him."

Joan nodded, but then turned to Sharon and asked, "So, I assume you know everything there is to know about your company?" Sharon looked at Joan, but didn't answer, and was glad when the starter signaled them.

Sharon and Joan both hit good drives right down the middle of the 1st fairway. As they walked off the tee, the storm that had been lingering out over the ocean moved in quickly. The two escaped to the clubhouse restaurant to wait and see if the rain might pass. After ordering iced tea, Joan, made it clear that her last question on the 1st tee was not a rhetorical one.

"Where did your company's stock close yesterday? Do you read your annual report? Don't most companies establish a few goals for the year? What are yours?"

Suddenly, instead of a student impressing the teacher with her 'A' knowledge, she felt like a dunce flunking a pop quiz. She felt she had also disappointed the teacher by not having ready answers.

Sharon shrugged. "I guess as long as my commission checks were good—and they were. Honestly, I saw no reason to pay any attention to the bigger picture. I'm just a galley slave—as long as I was being well-fed, I never made it my business to know where the ship was headed."

Joan corrected Sharon, "Not so much of a galley slave. More like a serf in the middle ages. Working your fields just fine, unaware of what the prince is up to—until one day, a foreign army shows up to steal your cattle. Suddenly the prince's problems are your problems."

"I guess you're right. I never really saw the company's problems as my problems. I was happy doing my own thing and never too worried about what was going on in the floors above mine. Now it looks like I may have to be concerned. I'm working harder to make less money and if I change jobs, that gap could get even wider."

"Often I've found if you work smarter, you don't have to work harder. But, then, nothing fails like success."

"What was that?"

"You see it all the time. People become complacent in their success. Stick to the old methods even if the game has changed. Stop looking for new challenges. You see it in businesses, sports teams. My brother was a career army officer and is a big military history buff. He spends part of every year in Gettysburg. That battle is one of his favorite topics for dinner table conversation, if you can believe that," Joan shook her head in disbelief.

"Over dinner?" Sharon puzzled.

"Oh, yes. I've heard him go on many times about how Robert E. Lee's big mistake at Gettysburg was to believe that *because he had never lost, he couldn't lose.* He ordered a charge that most of his subordinates said couldn't succeed. If he had listened, the whole war might have ended differently."

"How many times have you heard it said of some movie

star or athlete, as their career begins to crumble, they started believing their own press?" Sharon agreed. "While I was good enough at my job, I guess I thought I knew it all."

"The most important lessons I've learned in life were the ones I learned *after* I knew it all," Joan said with a smile.

"It's easy to get cocky when you're on top. And I was on top at my company for a long time, never looking at how I got there, or why I stayed there."

"You do want to keep your job, right?"

"If I can."

"If you really want to get the edge on the competition, it sounds to me like you're going to have to tell Jeff things about his own company that he doesn't know. And, I might add, learn a little bit more about yours as well."

"I'm embarrassed to admit I know so little about my own company."

"You're not alone. Think about it. We all prefer to live in ignorance. How many people can name their congressional representative? We think it doesn't concern us. Then when Washington passes a law we don't like, we scream, '*Who elected those people?*' Only when it impacts us do we make the effort to notice.

"Some find it easier to worry about sports' scores than the situation in Washington or on Wall Street, because basketball is something they understand. They really get confused with that other stuff. Yet, those who do have a pretty good grasp of what is going on are certainly well ahead of most. In the land of the blind, the one-eyed woman is queen."

Sharon nodded appreciatively.

"To quote Francis Bacon, '*Knowledge itself is power,*'" Joan said.

"Yeah, well, Francis may have to give me a job. I've been glancing at some of the job listings on the web and have actually started working on my resume this week. It's been years since I've looked at it, but that's how worried I'm getting."

"Why do you like to play golf?" Joan asked, puzzling Sharon with the sudden change of topic.

"It's fun."

"Is it? The last time we played, it looked like you were having more frustration than fun."

"I was, but that's part of the game."

"So if it were easy, you would not enjoy it as much?"

"I guess not."

"So it's not just to win?"

"No. It's not about the winning, per se. It's about the challenge. You and I aren't betting or anything, so it's not as though I beat *you* or anything…."

"So it's the challenge you like?"

"Yes. And not the challenge of playing you, since we hardly compare scores. More like challenging myself. Not being measured against you or by you, or anyone else. Just me testing myself. The greens and fairways and woods are just the playing field on which I do it. Even though I've played this course dozens of times, it's different every time, and the outcome's never certain."

"Coming up with your own unique solution to each new problem?"

"Exactly. And it's not as though I'm the only person who ever had to play their shot from the deep grass behind that rock, but I'm going to be the one playing it now. No one can help, or play it for me."

Sharon stopped and looked at Joan's smile, and wondered if they were still talking about golf. "So you think it's premature to start dusting off the resume?"

"I just question," Joan said, "whether your time is best spent sending out resumes and job hunting."

"There's only so much time in a day, and I guess I started wondering whether I should be job hunting, or researching a lost account."

"Is it lost? Until they sign a contract, there's still hope."

"But if Jeff knows so little about his own company's business strategy and priorities—not to mention he doesn't seem to care, then—"

"I think, then," Joan began, politely interrupting Sharon, "to really help Jeff, you need to do more than just ask him what they're up to. It sounds like you really care about Jeff, and that seems to me to be an important first step."

Sharon's brow furrowed. Sharon enjoyed Joan's company, but she had to admit part of the reason she took time out to golf with Joan was for the woman's sage advice. Now it seemed to be almost overwhelming. Her head was swimming as Joan kept talking.

"You need to go out on *your own* and do *your own* research to be able to bring some useful information back to him. It's like this round of golf. If I don't know what's beyond the dogleg, behind the trees, anymore than you do, asking me is not going to help either one of us. As much as I may want to help you, I can't—not if I don't know. Rather than asking me for information I don't have—or don't think I need—you would be better off doing your own homework and then coming back to me with information which helps us both. And beyond just what's out there, if you can figure out *how* to play it, that would really benefit us both."

Sharon nodded, trying to absorb everything Joan was saying.

"As someone once said, 'even if you are on the right track, if you just sit there, you'll get run over'. You have to ask yourself what you or your company can do for Jeff and his company that the other people can't. If you solve a key problem, Jeff will want to listen, but he will have to understand why that is a problem for *him*—not just the company. As humans we tend to be self-serving and are better motivated by things that impact us personally. Granted, we want to know how it will benefit the organization, but we are even more interested in 'what's in it for me.' He may only see his own end of things."

Joan went on, "If you know what goals Jeff's company set for this year, what problems it's having, and what problems keep its CEO or president awake at night, then you can see how all that fits in with what Jeff does."

Sharon smiled. "Maybe I have too much information."

"You can't have too much information. The one-eyed woman may be queen, but think of the power you wield if you have two eyes and binoculars to see what is far ahead of you. You just need to figure out how to use that knowledge. This merger may be the break you were looking for. How could the changes within Jeff's company perhaps change the way they do business?"

The storm moved on just as quickly as it had moved in. With the skies beginning to clear, they noticed the starter walking over to the first tee.

"I say we go find our drives and have some fun focusing on golf," Joan said with a smile.

Returning a smile and lifting her iced tea in a mock toast, Sharon replied, "To our game. The first one who talks about business again pays for snacks."

*   *   *   *   *   *   *   *   *   *   *   *

Sharon's first contact with Alan did not go well. He was in as bad a mood as she had ever seen him. When she asked Alan about SSI's company goals, he roughly told her to quit worrying about the company and start worrying about her job.

Sharon spent the rest of the week trying to buy time with Alan, while at the same time digging deeper into the inner workings of ToolTech. She asked questions of everyone she could about how ToolTech functioned and how they used her software. When she realized how limited the uses of her software were at ToolTech, she started checking into what other software packages they had and how those worked. She found that other than the basics, like word processing, no two departments shared the same system. Communication between departments was almost non-existent. This struck her as odd, until she questioned how little she knew about her own company, Software Solutions, Inc. Did she know if SSI was capable of producing anything but what it did?

She wandered the halls of SSI and into departments she had not visited since her tour of the building her first day on the job ten years ago. Rather than short *"hi-bye"* conversations in the halls, she, for the first time, really took the time to talk to her fellow sales reps to get their input. She learned that their problems were similar to hers. They were all losing sales, finding doors closed to them that once were sure sales, but none of them had a clue as to why or how to change the situation.

They all seemed resigned to working longer hours but selling less, until, like Craig, they found themselves out of a job. They were as frustrated as she was. Perhaps more so. Some were clueless that they were clueless. Some gave her the old explanation that, *"Business is cyclical. It'll bounce back—always has."* Craig had thought that. At least Sharon was aware that something was wrong. Some of her colleagues were in an even worse position, because, as Sharon had always heard said of someone with an addiction problem: Admitting you have the problem is the first and necessary step to solving it. Some of her fellow reps were in total denial. She at least knew she had a major selling problem.

Smiling her nicest smile, she talked her way into office after office to meet the people who actually wrote the software she sold. She found that the story of the "software delays" had lost something in translation when it was passed up from the software engineers to the senior engineer, to the "marketing liaison," to Alan, and then finally to her and her fellow sales reps. She then asked one engineer, Erick McDermot, why they were working on version 5.0 when it was just a newer version of their old software, which did not do nearly what ToolTech, or presumably her other clients, needed it to do?

He shrugged, "No one ever *specked* different requirements."

She was amazed that in less than an hour, she had explained to him what ToolTech needed and was well on her way to a solution. McDermot laughed, telling her that what she had in mind he could do in less time than it would take to make 5.0 work. Sharon was suddenly struck that it might be possible to create software tailored to her customer's needs rather than have the client bend their needs to the software.

"How is that possible?" Sharon asked.

"The average product's development time has shrunk from eighteen months a few years ago to as little as three months today. Computers themselves now design products. And, especially with software, you can have programs write programs for you. But they have a much more difficult time trying to fix and improve existing software."

Sharon furrowed her brow.

"Look at it this way, it's like trying to convert a horse and buggy into a Ferrari—while it's moving! The old version's up and running right now, and the people who're using it are not going to want to stop using it while we upgrade. So some of the stuff that we'd like to do, we simply can't—not and have it still work, or be able to overwrite the old version. It has to dovetail perfectly, or we'll have some mighty angry customers.

"It'd be faster and easier to just start from scratch. Build a Ferrari in the shop and present it to the customer to replace the buggy. But then it's not compatible with the horses they already have.

"So, we're stuck trying to make the buggy do all the things of the new sports cars, but without losing any of the features that make the horse and buggy operational now."

Sharon nodded. "I hadn't thought about that. I get clients saying, 'I heard about a new software that does such-and-such, why can't yours?'"

"So you see my point, and if I may continue that analogy, I would need to really know what it is you want to do. Look at it this way—if I wanted to compete with Ferrari, how would I go about that?"

"Take apart a Ferrari, see how it works, and improve it with additional features, but ideally, more economically."

"*If* we're talking about making sports cars. You just assumed that. But what if we're talking about competing in *transportation*? So, our horse and buggy competes."

"But not as well," Sharon interjected.

"It depends what you mean by *as well*. You just made a value judgment. Ever been down to the Gas Lamp District?"

"Yes, of course."

"Ever take one of those carriage rides?"

"No, but I always wanted to. It looks very romantic."

"Ah ha. So for *romantic* transportation, it may be *better* than a Ferrari."

"Point taken."

"We could also compete in transportation by making bullet trains or air planes—"

"Or," catching the spirit of the discussion, Sharon added, "pogo sticks."

"That meets certain criteria. Like the Ferrari it would be *fun* transportation—if that is what we decided we wanted."

"And it beats the Ferrari in price comparisons!" Sharon offered.

"But if the criteria were transportation for more that one person?"

"The Ferrari barely qualifies. Isn't it a two-seater?"

"So we may look at the bullet train. Or the jet. More expensive than a pogo stick, but if we have to move 300 people 2,000 miles…."

Sharon laughed. "I just had this image of three hundred people pogoing down the interstate!

Erick also laughed at the thought. When he stopped, he said, "So, you see what I'm getting at. I'll need a very specific idea of what it is you need."

"I think I have a very good idea. And I want to stop competing and start over from scratch. *We* will define the criteria according to ToolTech's needs."

"Sounds good to me."

"You said it could take close to six months to a year to make 5.0 work. If you were to scrap it, start over, given the little bit I've already told you, to create the software that my client could *really* use—not just what we've been selling them—how long do you think that would take? Ballpark."

Erick leaned so far back in his chair that Sharon began to worry he might fall over. He stared so intently at the ceiling above his cubicle, Sharon finally looked up to see if the answer was somehow printed on the acoustic tile.

Erick finally righted himself in chair, whistled through his teeth and said, "If we got the whole team on it, a few months, maybe."

"Really?"

"As I said, it's easier to start over than to keep gilding this tired old horse. And it would be great to work on something new. I gotta tell you, all of us here down in the dungeon are sick of this 4.0 and 5.0 stuff you guys keep selling."

"I sell it because you make it."

"If you don't want to sell, and I don't want to make it, and the customers don't want to buy it, then what are we doing?"

"It's because it's what we do."

"We do what we do because we do it," Erick restated. He thought for a moment and added, "I guess that's about it."

"Sometimes I think that's all there is to it. I was watching a thing about the Titanic on one of those education channels the other night with my son. Supposedly while the Titanic was going down, the busboys were clearing away dishes. They didn't know what else to do, so they did the only job they knew how to do. Well, I for one am tired of clearing away the dirty dishes as this ship sinks."

Erick smiled. "Are you launching a revolution? I thought us engineers were the only ones who were fed up. We have about thirty different nicknames for 5.0, none of which I can use in mixed company."

"Don't let my being female bother you."

"Oh, it's not because you're a woman. We've got lots of women down here. It's 'cause you're not an engineer. The women come up with some of the best names. As a salesperson, you just wouldn't get the joke."

"I sell software—," Sharon started to protest, a little defensively.

"It's not the same. You wouldn't get it. It just shows how differently you guys view the world than we do. I'll tell you a joke to illustrate my point. A salesman, a hardware guy and a software guy are driving along. The car gets a flat tire. The salesman says, 'Time to get a new car!' The hardware guy says, 'Let's swap the front wheel with the back wheel; that might fix it,' and the software guy says, 'Let's just restart the car and keep driving; it'll probably fix itself.'"

Sharon laughed. "Okay, point taken. I'll have to remember that one to tell my golf buddy."

Erick shook his head. "Tell that to someone who doesn't work in computers at all and they'll never get the joke."

"You're right," Sharon laughed again. "Now, if we really wanted to do this new software thing, how would we go about it?" She was getting excited that a plan was coming together, and that both she and her software would actually be of benefit to ToolTech.

"Obviously I can't start writing software without permission from somebody."

"At first I wouldn't need the actual software, just a very detailed outline of what it could do. A step-by-step plan."

Erick grimaced. "Even that would take a few days. I'd

need to talk to my boss."

"I understand. Do you want me to talk to him?"

"Her—Vicky Fong. Let me call her and ask her to step in here."

When Erick finished suggesting to Vicky that he stop working on 5.0 for a few days to work on Sharon's proposal, Vicky said, "And make us miss our deadline?"

Sharon frowned, thinking there was no chance, but then both Vicky and Erick could hold it no longer and both burst out laughing.

Sharon did not get the joke. When Erick stopped laughing, he had tears in his eyes. "Sorry, just one of those things you wouldn't understand."

Vicky chimed in, still laughing, "We've missed so many deadlines. And the people upstairs have made so many changes and set so many ridiculous new deadlines—without asking us how long it might take, or if we can even do what they suggested—we're so far behind on 5.0, that is has just become our running joke down here."

Erick continued, "If someone says they're going to lunch, someone else is likely to say, 'What?!?! You can't go to lunch! You'll make us miss our deadline!' You kind of have to live down here in the dungeon to appreciate it. We don't get enough light."

"I guess so," Sharon said, forcing a smile.

"Of course you can borrow Erick for a few days," Vicky concluded.

Sharon could not believe that suddenly she seemed on track to a solution; she knew that being on the right track was half the battle. She wanted to use everything she had learned about ToolTech's overall needs and SSI's capabilities to craft a software package which would bring out the best in both companies. Her conversation with Erick had brought about a distillation of what really needed to be done.

Sharon felt nervous hiding in engineering from Alan, but

she knew if her plan worked it would save her, Alan, and possibly Software Solutions itself. She spent the better part of her week doing a detailed outline with Erick of ToolTech's needs. He produced the specs she needed. Vicky looked them over to confirm that engineering could produce what Erick had outlined, and on the timetable he had created. Now that she had the backing of engineering, she set another golf date with Jeff. Just the two of them. Just a friendly game. For old time's sake, so she said. This time she knew she was bringing ammunition which would likely make Jeff view his job and all of ToolTech and SSI in a completely different light.

Playing out of the Rough

Once you have gathered useful information about your client, are you prepared to analyze and process that information to craft a solution?

- Do you know the performance issues for your customer's industry? At what do they have to excel at in order to be successful?

- Do you know your customer's business strategy to achieve growth and profitability?

- Can you craft a solution that will help the customer improve their position in the marketplace?

- Are you aware of the capabilities of your own organization? Do you know it's limitations and potential areas of unexplored growth?

Gathering information about your client can result in confusion—*if you don't know what to look for.* Sharon, with the help of Joan's questioning, begins to understand the key business performance issues for her client, ToolTech, and her own company, Software

Solutions, Inc. Understanding the economic performance requirements of her client, Sharon begins to identify the business problem. With a full understanding
of ToolTech's challenges, she then takes a look at her
resources to determine if SSI has the capability to
"build the solution."

Sharon is at a crossroads in her career. In the past, she
experienced success by being trustworthy and an
effective problem solver for her customers. In today's
competitive environment being trustworthy and an
effective problem solver is a given; she has to bring
solutions and ideas that give her customer a competitive advantage. Sharon must no longer view her role
as merely selling software, but as selling solutions;
Sharon must become a consultant.

CHAPTER FOUR

Changing your game

"It's good to see you, Sharon, but your phone calls have become a little strange lately. So I suspect we're here to do more than play golf," Jeff said as they approached the first tee.

"That's one of the things I've always liked about doing business with you—you get right to the point. Friendly, but concise," Sharon said, making a slicing motion with her hand.

"Time is money, even on the golf course," Jeff smiled as he pulled his driver from his bag. "At least for the pros."

"Well, there are a few things I'd like to discuss with you," Sharon answered as she reached into the side pocket of her golf bag for a few papers, quickly holding them up as proof, but returning them to her bag before he could really see them.

"I see." Jeff frowned. "You promised me on the phone that you understood that the decision has been made to go with LatCo.'s software. Frankly Sharon, LatCo isn't only cheaper—they're better. That's not a reflection on you, of course. I realize you don't make the stuff, but—"

Sharon held up the hand onto which she had just pulled her golf glove. "Say no more. I don't blame you for going with LatCo on this one, if you're just buying software. You're a smart man. You saw the advantages—minor though they were—and at a better price. Case closed. I'd lose all respect for you if you did otherwise. That's another reason I liked doing business with you, you always demanded the best."

"So what's all that paper? You're not going to keep score in triplicate, I assume."

"The way I've been hitting them lately, it would take several sheets of paper to tally my score!"

Jeff smiled and then shoved his tee into the ground and smacked a hard shot down the middle of the fairway. "I like this first hole on the North Course. A nice easy straightaway to get you started right." Then, turning to Sharon as she prepared to hit her drive, Jeff smiled and said, "It's not that I don't miss our golf games, Sharon, but I know you too well to think we're here for me to give you pointers on your backswing—as though I could."

Sharon hit her drive just a few yards short of his. "Don't need it—that one went straight," she smiled. "And, you're right. This hole may be the least picturesque at Torrey Pines, but it is a good warm-up. You're also right on another matter. This is not just about golf with an old friend. I wanted to talk to you about the traffic jams at CTC warehouses all over the country."

Jeff was so baffled by her comment that his driver missed the bag when he went to replace it. The siren of an ambulance on its way to the UCSD Medical Center echoed in the distance.

Sharon waited until the wail had completely subsided before she spoke again so that she would have Jeff's undivided attention. "Did you know that warehouse delays at CTC cost them over $2 million last year?" She hit her approach shot as casually as if she had just mentioned the lovely weather, then turned back to Jeff. "And warehouse problems at ToolTech, your own company, often result in double-orders, double-shipments, and incomplete shipments, which not only makes ToolTech look bad, but costs the company money. One of the goals they established for this year was to cut shipping costs by 20 percent."

Sharon casually traded her 7-iron for the putter in her bag. "It's expensive. And when ToolTech buys out CTC, what's going to happen? Take Texas for example, each company has a warehouse in Dallas and each has a warehouse in Houston. It won't make sense for the new company to have two warehouses in each city, but they won't be able to close them down when they need all that warehouse space just to stockpile duplicate orders and partial shipments waiting for the rest of the order."

Jeff stood over his ball but was too mesmerized by Sharon's enthusiasm to remember to do anything but listen.

"Your shot," she said, with great nonchalance. Sharon waited until Jeff hit his sloppy shot, too intent on listening to her to focus on his game. She continued, "If you had software that could coordinate all aspects of the business from your purchases for production, all the way through production, and could automatically notify Butterman to ship when the order is ready to go, then—"

"Butterman?" Jeff asked in surprise, almost sorry to interrupt her flow.

Sharon walked to the far side of the green and watched Jeff carry his wedge into the bunker on the right side of the green. The club car stopped and the eager young woman driving it asked if they needed drinks or sandwiches. They both declined and the snack bar-on-wheels sped off.

"Butterman?" Jeff asked again.

"Butterman," Sharon repeated. "J.J. Butterman in Portland, Oregon. They make your stands."

"I didn't—"

"Don't worry, no reason you should've. I've been doing a lot of research—on the web, reading industrial magazines, talking to people. Anyway, ToolTech and CTC both subcontract with Butterman. Butterman then ships the stands to Houston, Dallas, Pittsburgh, Baltimore—any of your warehouses. The stands are repackaged and added to the set of cartons. The cartons are then shipped to your customers. Makes zero sense.

"We tie your computers into Butterman's. Butterman ships the stands to arrive the same day as the equipment."

Jeff blinked at Sharon.

"I know what you're thinking," Sharon smiled, enjoying his bewilderment. "No one is supposed to know that ToolTech or CTC subcontract. The Butterman name never appears on anything. Still doesn't have to. The shipping labels and cartons can all say ToolTech. With the merger, no one will even wonder why the stands are now coming from Portland instead of the local warehouse."

"Actually, I didn't—," Jeff began.

"I know. No one does. It's okay. It's still your shot. You're still away," Sharon concluded. "I just need to putt."

"This is all fascinating, but, why tell *me* about warehouse problems in Houston?"

Sharon smiled. "Your company is going to have to buy software from someone. And wouldn't it make more sense to buy it from a software company that can guarantee that the software can interface with every other bit of software from production, shipping and all up and down the line? Software that can communicate with your suppliers' computers, *and* tell the folks at the warehouse in Houston what orders will be coming so they can prepare space? Software that could even automatically email each of your transportation subcontractors, like Mathias & Sons in Houston, how big a shipment, and on what day? Did you know that shipments often sit for days blocking the loading dock at the Houston warehouse—without trucks or drivers—because no one thinks to notify Mathias?"

Jeff shook his head, still dumbfounded. It took him three attempts to clear the sand and he was still not on the green. "How do you—"

"I've been checking. Talked to your warehouse manager here in San Diego, and a couple of ToolTech's truck drivers at the coffee shop they go to. Made a couple calls to Houston. The rest was simple Internet and library research. You'd be amazed at the amount of information on the web."

Jeff finally scooped his ball onto the edge of the green with his wedge. "That's all very impressive, Sharon, and it sounds great, all but for one thing. Why're you telling *me*? I buy for the hardware division of ToolTech. Period. I think it's great that you have taken such an interest in my company, but what their cartons say or where they ship from is really not any concern of mine. I can't agree more that it's stupid our products sit on loading docks for lack of transportation. But my concern is what, when, and how much material comes *in*—not what *leaves* or *how*. "

"It's not your concern? Jeff, I used to think SSI's problems didn't concern me. Now I could be out of a job any day. SSI is shrinking its sales force. What they do very much concerns me all of a sudden."

"Wow, I didn't know things were that bad."

"They're getting there," Sharon said as she dropped her three-foot putt. "Something you should think about—when ToolTech buys CTC, how many purchasing people will the new corporate-giant need?"

Jeff missed his eight-footer and frowned at Sharon as he walked past the hole. "Sure there have been rumors that a few people's jobs will have to shift or—"

"Rumors? Shift? Did you know that when CTC took over Somerset Tool in '93, they brought in Scott, David & Associates to plan the restructuring—"

"But as I recall, they only let about four hundred people go, and with two big companies like that—"

"All but a handful of those lay-offs were in middle management, in departments like purchasing and HR. That's always where Scott, David recommends cuts. They've already been hired by ToolTech to start examining—"

"Even so," Jeff said picking up his ball without even bothering to putt it in. "Give me a ten or something. Even so, this is out of my department."

"Is it going to be enough to try not to lose your job, or are you going to have to fight to keep it?"

"How did you do on that hole?" Jeff asked.

"Birdie."

Jeff smiled weakly.

"I am not trying to scare you and maybe things aren't that

bad, but I have learned a few things you may want to think about."

"Please, go on," Jeff requested.

Walking toward the second hole, they could see they had caught up with what appeared to be a senior womens' league. Sharon knew there would be a considerable wait and decided to make the most of their time. Jeff listened as he looked down the divot-scarred fairway.

Sharon continued, "I mean, it may be playing it safe to do what you've always done, but is that going to be enough to stand out in this mega-corporation you guys are building and will it impress the boys upstairs enough to keep *you* around when the smoke clears? If I were to play the club pro, for money, should I play it safe and try to play my usual game? If I do—guaranteed, I lose. Right? My only chance, and I do mean *only* chance, would be to take some big risks, play aggressively, and gamble that I'll make enough of those risky shots to win. Playing it safe sometimes isn't really safe; it's just slower defeat."

Jeff studied Sharon, but said nothing, so Sharon continued. "I ran into your wife at soccer. Our sons' teams were playing each other. She said you had your daughter at a Little League baseball game. It's hard to keep up with these kids, isn't it?"

Jeff nodded. "I'm supposed to be coaching her baseball team, but most of the time, I'm not sure who's running the show."

Sharon shook her head. "I feel bad. I've only made a couple of my son's games this year. Jackie mentioned you just got your son into that private school." Then, suddenly zeroing in on her point of emphasis, Sharon brought her point home. "Even if you don't lose your job, are you going to want to be transferred to Austin?"

With his head down, staring at the ground, Jeff nodded in understanding.

"One of the things I stumbled across on the web was that

CTC just built a new industrial park there. They had half of it up for rent, but then took it off the market. Sounds like they're going to use it themselves. If ToolTech merges its operations with CTC's, are you ready to pick up and move?

"You told me that since Ann was promoted over you, the two of you are like North and South Korea—not open warfare, but there's no love lost there, either. If she has to pick someone to transfer or get rid of, look around your department and ask yourself, *'If I were Ann who would I pick?'*"

All trace of a smile was gone from his face. Sharon noticed that the group of older women playing ahead of them were making little progress. Jeff seemingly stared into space.

Realizing she had already given him too much to mull over, Sharon decided to begin again—only this time, with a little more sympathy. "It's just that Ann knows as well as you do that you should've had her job. I think it makes her nervous to have you around. Makes her feel like a coup is imminent, even if you're not plotting."

"I'm not—," Jeff began, but Sharon nodded understandingly and waved him off, so he paused.

Sharon nodded sympathetically. "My boss—you remember Alan?—and I are not exactly best buds these days, either. When things start looking gloomy, everyone wants someone to blame, or someone beneath them to take it out on. You know that old continuum—I think I learned it in a management class when I was getting my MBA: Your co-workers can go quickly from supportive to non-supportive. Alan has just slipped from neutral to non-supporter," Sharon said with a laugh. "And is falling fast."

Jeff nodded, laughing, "And Ann on a good day is non-supporting. On a bad day she's putting viruses into my computer!"

Sharon shook her head, "Oh, she's not that bad."

"I know, I'm joking. But you're right. Ann and I are no longer the chums we were when we shared an office. We always had lunch, told jokes. Now—I can't remember the last time we talked about anything not absolutely essential to the job."

"It's not all her fault. Ann is in over-her-head, and she knows it. And with this merger looming like a storm front on the horizon, I suspect tornado warnings will be in effect around your office for quite some time to come. You know how dicey things can go with these big acquisitions. In-fighting and turf-battles have killed or weakened some pretty big companies in acquisitions."

A Navy helicopter WHUMP-WHUMPED low overhead. Jeff watched it hug the coast and then stared in silence at his driver as though it somehow held the answers. "I can already see people jockeying for position and maneuvering to try to be on top when the two trains collide. I sort of thought as long as I stayed out of the way and kept a low profile, I'd be okay. Now, you've got me thinking…." Finally he looked up. "How did you know…. Well, never mind. What are you proposing?"

"Excuse me," one of the older women cooed. "Would you like to play through? We'll probably slow you down."

Jeff said, "No," and Sharon, "Yes," simultaneously. Sharon looked at him.

Jeff stood up and slipped his driver into his bag. "I'd rather go back to the clubhouse and look over what you brought. Do you mind?"

"Not at all," Sharon replied. "Thank you, ladies, but I think we'll be getting coffee."

*   *   *   *   *   *   *   *   *   *   *   *

At the clubhouse, the two sat at a table among a sea of papers. The waiter had refilled their coffee cups at least three times, but other than nodding a perfunctory *thank you,* Jeff had not said a word. Sharon had said only small things, such as, "Here," when handing Jeff another stack of sheets. They were the only two in the restaurant that early in the day. For almost two hours the waiter watched Jeff intently read document after document.

Finally Jeff stood up and walked over to the windows, stared out at the 1st tee and watched two brightly clad men drive balls down the fairway. Jeff stretched and walked back to the table.

"Wow," he said, rubbing his hands on the back of his neck. "Wow. Half the time I find myself guessing at how many units of what to buy. Under your new system, I, and all of purchasing, would know exactly how many of what to buy, when. This is amazing."

Sharon smiled.

"You've done your homework—and then some. I had no idea. And I know I've just glimpsed at the tip of the iceberg."

"Yep. Plenty more where that came from."

"I'm not sure I could handle any more. My head is about to explode." Jeff rubbed his eyes again. "It's going to take me a while to digest the rest of this."

"I understand. I brought copies for you to take."

"Bottom line. What do you want to do with all of this? You know that selling this plan—integrated software across the full spectrum of ToolTech, CTC and their suppliers—is going to take a green light that I can't give."

"But you agree it's a good idea?"

"It's a great idea. But it's way over my head."

"I realize that."

"And Ann isn't going to want to even hear about this. We just had two of your biggest competitors take up almost a full day of both of our time—supposedly some great new software. This major dog-and-pony show with bells and lights and whistles turned out to be just the newest version of the same old stuff all dressed up. Ann and I were both quite annoyed that they wasted our time. It was the first thing we had agreed on in months. And we're still planning to go with LatCo, so it didn't change anything. She is going to be very reluctant to sit through another pitch no matter how good."

Sharon nodded sympathetically. "Whether she'll go for it or not, I think as common courtesy, you should at least try Ann first. And, who knows, she might surprise you." Jeff tilted his chin, slightly raising his eyebrows to offer a doubtful look. Sharon smiled at his exaggerated reaction and then continued, "However, if I understand your organizational chart, this is too big a decision for her anyway."

"Yes, and frankly, I wouldn't hold your breath on Ann being our stepping stone. I don't think she will want to take the time to understand it."

"From what you've told me of her, I'd have guessed that. That's why I ultimately want to see the VP of operations, Bill Atkinson."

Jeff stared numbly. "You want to see Bill Atkinson?"

"Yes."

"Do you know Bill Atkinson?"

"No."

"I didn't think so. No one knows Bill Atkinson. Bill Atkinson speaks only to Cabots and the Cabots only to God."

"Huh?" Sharon's brow furrowed.

"Never mind. Just an old saying about Boston blueblood families not wanting to associate with the riffraff. No one gets to see Bill Atkinson. I think his wife has to make an appointment a year in advance."

"He's not married," Sharon interjected.

"See?!? No one knows anything about the man! Except you—I know. You seem to know everything. I swear you've been following me. This report is incredible. I can't wait until I get to the part about what kind of sandwich I packed in my daughter's lunch this morning!"

"P.B. and J," Sharon said, smirking.

Jeff's jaw dropped. "You're starting to scare me!"

"Jackie," Sharon laughed, "said she had to stop after the

game for jelly. Said Heather is in the," Sharon imitated a five-year-old, "'If I can't have peanut butter and jelly I would rather starve' phase."

Jeff let out a laughing sigh. "Don't do that again, you're starting to worry me!"

"Just want to be prepared—well armed with information for the assault on Bill Atkinson's fortress of solitude."

"When you start peeking in my windows, I'll get a restraining order!" Jeff joked.

He looked back down at the papers in front of them. "So you want to see Bill Atkinson. Tall order. I think I could get an audience with the Pope with less trouble. But, I'll do my best."

"My friend Joan told me that during World War II Winston Churchill said, 'Sometimes it is not enough to do your best. Sometimes you have to do whatever is required.' I've never seen you back away from a challenge."

"I didn't say I wouldn't do it—I just said it wouldn't be easy. The 'difficult' I can do immediately; the 'impossible' may take a few days."

"Don't take too long. LatCo is supposed to get the contract next week, and it'll be a lot harder to get anyone to listen after that money has been spent," Sharon warned.

"I know, but I think I can hold things up a week or two, maybe, to buy us more time."

"I think this is a good idea that could profit us both, but I don't want you getting in trouble at work."

"Sharon, I really appreciate your bringing this to me. This all makes so much sense; I don't know why no one ever thought of it before."

Sharon left money on the table, far more than a few cups of coffee could possibly cost as a sizable tip. The two continued their discussion as they left the restaurant.

"Anything else you want me to do?" Jeff asked jokingly.

"Well, I have this idea for turning lead into gold...."

Jeff laughed, but as they walked toward their cars he said,

"I'm not sure how easy this is going to be. To get everyone to see the logic...."

"I know it won't be easy, but look at it this way—I gain very little by taking credit for all this research inside your company. As much as you want, you can make it look like *your* digging and *your* idea."

"It isn't though. In fact, I wasn't very helpful when you called looking for information."

"I don't care about that. I wasn't looking at the big picture, either. You see the value now and that's all that matters. Even I didn't know what I wanted then. It took me a while to see what information I needed, what it all meant and how to make it work for us. I spent a lot of sleepless nights trying to get this to come together into a plan of action."

"It was worth it. It is a great idea."

"Now that I have the information, we can use it to benefit us both. All this knowledge is useless without your taking advantage of it. You have to be a big part of this, or I get nowhere. It'll be *your* information by the time you digest it to the point necessary to sell the people at your company. I wouldn't even be on this track if you hadn't made yourself so accessible over the years and cared enough about your job to take an interest. You were impressed when you saw the level of detail, right? He will be, too."

"But what if he doesn't go for it?"

"It still doesn't make you look bad. Even if he says no, which I can't believe he will, he'll still have to take note of the fact that you're a thoughtful, innovative sort of guy. With all the reshuffling that is bound to happen when the CTC people come on board, it will be helpful to have someone up above know you as more than just a name on a company directory."

"True."

"It'll be harder for Ann to fire you, or transfer you, if you're suddenly Bill Atkinson's fair-haired boy."

"Thanks, Sharon."

"Thank you, Jeff. One favor, though?"

"What's that?"

"I obviously have put a lot of time and effort into this…."

"That's for sure."

"So I don't want it to fall into the wrong hands—for any of my competitors to see."

"I understand," Jeff said.

"Good. Together, we're going to make this thing work for both of us."

Changing your game

Are you product-focused
or customer-focused as a salesperson?

- Can you quantify the potential economic business value of your solution to the customer's organization?
- Will your primary contact person sponsor you for business meetings with higher-level managers and executives and other relevant cross-functional people?
- Can you marshal appropriate resources from your own organization that have the power and ability to customize solutions for your customer?

Sharon learns of major changes within ToolTech that provide her with an opportunity to help them implement a solution that will achieve their stated business goal of reducing shipping costs by 20 percent. In this instance, her solution will result in an annual savings of $2 million. Often, major changes within a customer's organization, such as mergers, acquisitions, or technology shifts, are tremendous opportunities for salespeople to actively participate in solutions that usually have a highly quantifiable impact on the customer's business.

Many of these solutions require a major investment on the part of the buying organization thereby requiring salespeople, like Sharon, to access and gain the support of senior executives.

This "customer focus" requires salespeople to be able to customize solutions for their clients that can be delivered by the supplying organization.

CHAPTER FIVE

Course Management

The rain clouds hovered threateningly overhead as Sharon got her clubs out of the car. She double-checked to make sure her poncho and umbrella were in her bag. Joan suggested they get a cart so if the rain came they could race back to the club-house.

"So, Sharon, how'd it go with Jeff?"

Sharon scowled and shook her head.

Joan tsk-tsked. "From that look, I'd have to guess things didn't go well."

Sharon frowned at Joan and kept walking as the starter immediately signaled them.

"The meeting with Jeff went great. He was eager, even interested. And then his meeting with his boss was a complete fizzle. She didn't even want to hear word one. So Jeff went right to the VP himself."

Joan drew her driver, and with a nod, Sharon gave her honors. She pulled out her own club and continued talking. "Jeff couldn't even get in the door. Everyone these days wants to bypass the little guys and go straight to the head-honcho, so this guy in particular has become some kind of hermit. Jeff says the VP's secretary is known as the 'pit bull' for the tenacity with which she guards her boss' privacy."

Joan smiled, "I've known a few people like that in my day. At least you haven't lost your sense of humor about it."

"What was it Abraham Lincoln said, '*I laugh because I must not cry*'? And I have plenty to cry about. My boss is more upset than ever, and I can't say as I blame him. I was his star. His '*go-to guy*' as he used to put it. He counted on me, and now I feel like I've let him, and myself, down. He wants me to start turning in weekly progress reports. I haven't done that since I was a new rep on probation. I do a sort of informal version for myself, of course, but to have to start filling out those forms again...." Sharon shook her head and sighed.

Joan patted her on the shoulder as they walked to the tee.

"I can understand him wanting to look over my shoulder. I've been working my tail off, but without results, and that's all he sees. I forecasted Jeff's business as a big part of my budget this quarter. Without that sale, I've got nothing. Like a weather forecaster who keeps predicting rain that never comes, my credibility is lacking right now."

Joan shook her head sympathetically once again.

"I can understand him wanting to do it, but I don't like it. He always trusted me to do a good job, and I did. The best. He left me alone, and I liked it that way." Then, with a sigh, Sharon continued. "Now I'm thinking, maybe too much alone. We really don't have too much of a relationship. Without this sale to Jeff's company, I don't think I have a job."

Joan's drive was an instant replay of a few dozen short but straight drives right down the middle of the fairway on the number 1 par 4.

Sharon's frustrations seemingly transferred to her club. She barely topped the ball off the tee and it rolled down the mound. Sharon shook her head, looked at Joan, and laughed.

"Take a mulligan," Joan offered.

Sharon hesitated.

"We're here to have fun, there's no one behind us. We're not really keeping score...."

Sharon looked around. The course was rather empty on such a chilly day. She walked to her bag, unzipped a side pocket and pulled out a new ball.

"If the sale to Jeff is that important, and it sounds like it is, maybe you ought to offer Jeff a mulligan," Joan suggested.

Joan waited in silence as Sharon hit a replacement drive. It was not a great drive, but it was much better than the first. Sharon retrieved her flubbed first ball; then they climbed in the cart and Joan took off. The cart bounced along so fast that they sped past Sharon's ball. Sharon pointed this out and Joan made a high-speed U-turn that would have made any bootlegger proud. "Sorry about that," Joan said. "I just love taking the whoop-dee-doos on that stretch of asphalt."

Sharon laughed at the childlike joy Joan seemed to take from simple things, mentally noting that simply being around Joan lifted her own spirits.

Sharon used her 5-iron and the ball shot off the club straight toward the green and stopped right on the fringe of the putting surface "Attagirl," Joan cheered. "You're back in the groove." Joan took out a 5-wood and proceeded to hit the ball in a high, arching shot that landed just before the green and rolled up about 15 feet from the cup. "Great shot!" yelled Sharon. Then, joking, she said, "You just won't let me win a hole, will you?"

"Just lucky," offered Joan with a smile. The two boarded the cart and rode up to the green.

Sharon was first to putt. After taking a good read of the green, Sharon stroked the ball from about 30 feet and it rolled toward the cup, stopping on the lip of the hole. Sharon groaned, "Fall in," but the ball didn't move and she tapped it in for a par. Joan lined up her putt and stroked the ball, pulling it a little left, missing the cup by about two inches. She carefully tapped the ball into the hole.

"Two pars! That hasn't happened very often. Hope we've started a trend," said Joan with laughter in her voice.

Still relishing the moment, the two walked to the golf cart and replaced their clubs in their bags. Joan quickly whirled them away to their second tee.

"It seems that you've found that 'zone,' where you are relaxed and focused," commented Joan. "Golf seems to mirror life in that our mental state shows up in our performance in every aspect of day to day living."

"You know, I think you're right. Though I'm still concerned for my job, I'm not nearly as uptight as I was several weeks ago. At least now, I have a tentative solution for Jeff's company. And, for that alone, I feel better. Of course, in my situation, what choice did I have," said Sharon with a half-hearted laugh. "I either reinvented my approach or hit the road."

"There's that line in *Star Wars* where Yoda says, '*Do or not do. There is no try.*'"

Sharon stopped for a moment to laugh. "I wouldn't have taken you for a *Star Wars* fan."

"I have grandchildren, remember?"

"That's right. It makes me feel old that I can remember so well when it first came out, and now my son sees it like some kind of a classic."

"And don't you find that when you watch old movies with him it gives you a new perspective?"

"Sure does," agreed Sharon. "You see things you never saw before, or in a way you never saw them."

"As on a golf hole. Even though lots of other people have studied the hole, you have to see it fresh for yourself and make your own conclusions. Should I drive left and miss the trap but have a safe position on the fairway, or swing away and trust I can clear the sand?"

"And a lot of that is evaluating the downside risk," added Sharon.

"That's true," said Joan. "A lot of golf is really risk assessment and mistake management. Each shot is not going to land exactly where you planned. So when it doesn't, what are you going to do about it? With this work thing, you've really got nothing to lose. Suggest a different approach to Jeff and ask him to try again. You've done all this work and made all of this progress, are you going to give up now?"

"I'm afraid if I keep bugging Jeff it will ruin our friendship. I've gotten to know him and his wife and family rather well over the years."

"First of all, you said the friendship may be ruined anyway, right? Didn't you say that since he's not been buying from you that he feels so awkward being around you that the friendship is already strained? Sadly, it sounds like if you don't salvage the business with him, you may not be able to save the friendship, either.

"Secondly, you shouldn't look at it as 'bugging' Jeff. From what you've said, you are fighting for his job as much as yours. His situation may not be as desperate as yours, but it does sound like he agrees that the merger could shake things up a lot for him. Your plan could do a lot to enhance his position.

"It appears you could best serve your and Jeff's interests by making this plan work for both of you and for both of your companies. You've come this far. I say you owe it to yourself and Jeff to give it one more try."

Joan continued talking, as she stopped the cart at the second tee. "I used to play golf with a retired nun. She would always pray to Saint Anthony to help her find her lost golf balls. Not being Catholic, I asked why. She said basically, that God is busy and you could pray to certain saints who sort of specialized in certain things, and ask them to intervene on your behalf. Get one of them to carry your message to the head guy. If you can't talk to the man at the top yourself—or I should say, if Jeff can't—then find someone who has the big man's ear and talk to them."

Sharon smiled. "That makes sense. I don't know why I didn't think of that. I've made many a sale by pitching my story to an administrative assistant while the boss was too busy to see me."

"And it always seemed to work for Sister Connie. I never saw her lose a ball. Of course, she was eighty-four and couldn't hit them more than a few yards—but she never lost a ball."

Sharon laughed.

"Think of trying to get close to the top as a 'lag' putt. You probably won't putt it all the way into the cup the first time, but you try to get it close enough that it's easy to make on the next shot."

Sharon and Joan waited while the foursome playing in front of them searched for a missing ball.

"Basically, what you're saying is that I need to find some way to get one step closer to the VP of operations. But how?"

"See if you can go wide—find someone else who sees your solutions as critical to their success," explained Joan.

"Easier said than done, but I'm game," remarked Sharon, still trying to follow Joan's advice.

"If I understand your new plan, you'll find yourself not just meeting the people you have always done business with, like your friend Jeff—informally, on the golf course—but soon having to present your ideas to the suits in the boardroom. And you may have to figure out a way to talk to anyone in between who can get you access to the next rung above."

Sharon nodded. "I'm already seeing that. Actually, it's as though I'm becoming much more of a sales consultant than a sales rep." Joan smiled as she noticed a look of determination beginning to spread across Sharon's countenance.

Sharon went on, "And, if I have to sell to the suits in the boardroom, then that's just what I'll do. I'm convinced I can help them achieve a major cost reduction—one that was promised to the board in order to sell the merger." Then, with a sigh, Sharon continued. "The problem is getting to see the people at the planning level."

"True. But there is more than one way to play any hole. You could use a putter all the way, like I saw—I think it was Billy Casper—do during a windstorm at Pebble Beach. He took about four strokes to make a short par three. But he did the best of anyone on the hole after watching other guys take sevens or eights, with the wind whipping drive after drive onto the rocks or into the water. He putted off the tee and down the cart path, all the way to the hole. It kept his shots below the wind. Be creative. Try a different approach."

"Are you suggesting a sneaky side-entrance?"

"It's not sneaky. There are people who have power out of proportion to their rank. Who really has more power, the First Lady, or some freshman congressman from Iowa? He can talk about childcare or drug abuse or beautifying the highways until he turns blue, but if the First Lady gives a speech about it—Wham!—it makes the evening news and suddenly we have a national childcare crisis. Jeff may make more money and *out-rank* that pit bull on any organizational chart of their company, but who really has more power? Who gets to see the head honchos on a daily basis?"

"You mean we may have to sell the pit bull first?"

"Perhaps. Or, more likely, find someone who can by-pass her altogether."

More to herself than Joan, Sharon mumbled, "We need an ally with access." As the foursome finally cleared Sharon and Joan readied to hit their tee shots. Sharon could see it raining out over the ocean. Joan suggested they make a run for it back to the clubhouse. As they sped off, Sharon looked toward Sorrento Valley, where her office was. She could see a break in the clouds.

*　*　*　*　*　*　*　*　*　*　*　*

At home that evening, Sharon once again found herself studying ToolTech. As Max said goodnight, she reflected how, ironically, her twelve-year-old had helped her learn more about ToolTech or CTC or Software Solutions than three-fourths of any of those companies' employees. She was amazed that she had blissfully lived in ignorance for so long.

The next morning she didn't bother to go into the office, but called Jeff as soon as she knew he would be at his desk.

"I don't know Lorenzo Ortiz. The name is vaguely familiar, but—," Jeff protested.

"He's the head of transportation at ToolTech. I've been studying the situation, and he, or I should say, his department, has the most to gain from our software development plan. I've identified the people at your company that control the key areas we can help, and he is one of them. And, he reports directly to Atkinson. He must know him and be able to see him."

"If I don't know Ortiz, I'm quite sure he's never even heard of me."

"I've thought about that. And how awkward it'd be for you to get him to see us so that we can share these ideas. So I have a plan. It's a little devious, but it'll give us the time we need to make him listen and pique his interest."

"How devious? This isn't going to get me fired or arrested, is it? You're not going to have me snooping in windows, are you?" Jeff joked.

"Possibly," Sharon deadpanned. "Just kidding! No, not at all. In fact, if you find any part of this objectionable, let me know. I don't want to do anything that could backfire on you—or me for that matter—later. It's nothing bad, I just want you to invite him for a round of golf. My friend Joan asked me to get together a foursome for a charity golf outing she is chairing."

"Does Ortiz play?"

"He does. Is one of the top players at his country club, actually."

"Sharon, how could you possibly know that? Have you started stalking my fellow employees?"

"Yeah, right," Sharon laughed. "There's a web site that has a golf handicapping system and lists players and their country clubs. Then I took a look at the homepage for his club and found he has won a few of their in-house tournaments."

"You're becoming quite the little cyber-junkie, aren't you? You'll have to give me the web address for that handicapping site."

"I'll email it to you. But right now, I'd like you to get in touch with Ortiz. Tell him you need a fourth for this charity thing and that you've heard he's good, and that since it's best-ball, you want him on your team. Stroke his ego a bit. Suggest we go out for a quick nine after work some night and get to know each other, and each others' strengths and weaknesses. Our fourth won't be able to make it."

"Who's our fourth?"

"We don't have one yet, but I'll scare one up before the tournament. While we play, you can ask me what I've been up to. I can casually tell you about a plan I'm developing for another one of my clients to integrate all of their departments, from receiving to shipping. It's all true. I'm working on plans for another customer besides ToolTech. You know I wouldn't ask you to lie. You tell me about all the problems ToolTech is having in that regard and how things are only going to get worse when they merge with CTC."

"Using your information. That's the devious part," Jeff chuckled.

"It's not completely devious. You told me you had done a little checking on your own after reading my material—you can just share more of that information with me. If nothing else, Ortiz will be impressed that you've done your homework and take such an interest in your company."

"You mean, *you*'ve done my homework," Jeff laughed again.

"Minor details."

"That's the way I made it through school, too. Always got the class brain to do my homework for me."

Sharon laughed, "Regardless of the source, you did take an interest. After you tell me about the problem, you can casually ask if maybe SSI might have something to solve ToolTech's and CTC's problems."

"And, let me guess, you just might," Jeff laughed.

"Well, funny you should ask...," Sharon joined him in a

chuckle. "And, if Ortiz is half the logistics-chief he is a golfer, he'll understand the potential impact."

"And if not?"

"Worse case scenario: You score major brownie points with Ortiz and you make a great connection to someone in senior management at your company. If things go any worse with Ann, you may need a mentor in another department."

"True."

"And Ortiz is a legitimate two-handicap. With him on our side, the least you will get out of this is a bronze plaque commemorating your victory at the golf tournament."

"Sharon, you're too funny. And after we're both fired we can sit around staring at our hard-earned trophies! I can't make any promises, but I'll try to set things up with Ortiz, ASAP."

"Good. I'm 99 percent sure he'll jump at the golf thing. If not, I have a plan B."

"Swell," Jeff joked, "but since it probably involves breaking into Atkinson's house, I don't want to hear about it until after this plan fails."

"Jeff, don't be negative. It won't fail. I have faith in you. And in us. We can make this happen."

*   *   *   *   *   *   *   *   *   *   *   *

Ortiz slipped his putter into his bag after sinking a fifteen-foot putt for par, his fourth par in four holes. "Jeff," he began, "it sounds like you've done some serious research."

"I try to keep up on things," Jeff beamed.

"This isn't really the time or place for all of this shop talk, however. When I play golf, I like to play golf. Forget about work. Sounds like you spend every waking hour thinking about the office. Lighten up. Enjoy life. When I'm at work, I work hard. Give the company 100 percent, and when I play, I play hard. I don't know of anyone who on their deathbed, said, *'Gee, if I'd only spent more time at the office.'"*

Jeff's smile slipped off his face.

"But," Ortiz continued, "you have raised some interesting points. You've told me things I didn't know about my own department. I assume you have data to back all this up?"

"Yes, of course," Jeff said, perking up again.

"I do like to keep work in the office. I have a full day of meetings tomorrow, so can you meet before work? Say seven, tomorrow morning, my office?"

"You've got it."

"And now, Sharon, so we can put all of this work behind us, you say you're confident this software integration will work for our company? I'd like to hear more about that. How soon do you think you could come up with an idea of what you could do for ToolTech?"

Sharon paused briefly to think of an appropriate answer that didn't make this golf game look like an ambush. She already had solid ideas, but knew giving him the full plan immediately would be a move that might appear over pre-pared at this stage. But, she also knew she couldn't wait long since the deal with LatCo was to be signed next week.

Ortiz mistook her pause. "I don't need complete specs. Just a good blueprint to show some people what we're talking about and what you're capable of doing."

"I could have something for you in, say, two days," said Sharon.

Ortiz appeared surprised, but nodded appreciatively. "I'm playing with a couple of workaholics. Anything else you two want to say about work?"

Jeff and Sharon looked at each other and both shook their heads.

"Good, because the next one who opens his *or her* mouth about anything work-related buys the food at the end of nine."

* * * * * * * * * * * *

74

At a lunch meeting three days later, Ortiz broke the bad news to Sharon and Jeff. "Sharon, the plan you sent me was great. Amazing detail. The cost savings will be terrific, unfortunately Atkinson won't even see me."

Jeff and Sharon's jaws both dropped. Sharon began, "But aren't you...."

"Yes. We exchange memos, and I see him once, twice a year, if I'm lucky. I asked his secretary for an appointment, and she refused. I feel stupid and childish telling you I can't even get to see my boss."

Sharon's eyes lit up. "So Mr. Atkinson didn't shoot down the idea?"

"He never heard the idea."

"You mean the pit bull—," Jeff began before Sharon cut him off.

"Did you tell her why you wanted to see him?"

"Yes, of course. That I had an idea to save the company some money."

Sharon shook her head.

Ortiz shrugged and went on, "She says he's too busy planning the merger to talk to me right now."

"From what I've read," Sharon began, "Atkinson has sort of been charged with making this merger work. According to the *Journal* and *Tool Time Monthly,* your chairman promised the shareholders all sorts of things to secure the votes to get the deal to go through. He then turned to your president, Mr. Gregory, and said, *'Make it happen.'* Gregory then turned to Atkinson and said, *'Fix this.'* So basically, Atkinson is the one who has to find the cost savings to make this merger the good deal your chairman promised it would be for everyone.

"No offense, Lorenzo, but *some money* is a vague term. In sales, I learned a long time ago, you need to be very specific. How much money? *Some* money could be $200 or $2 million. What's the profit in it for *him*?

"Would you do all of us a favor and try again? Leave Mr.

Atkinson a message giving him the answer to one key question: How we can cut his shipping costs by 20 percent this year, in keeping with the goals he set. And see if he doesn't get back to you."

Ortiz nodded appreciatively.

"Actually I think we can do better than 20 percent, but start with quoting his number. He'll know we've read his analysis. Even if we just leave it at 20 percent, that's almost $2 million, the first year, which pays for the software. That doesn't even count the savings in other departments and in years to come! Not to mention the additional $2 million CTC will save in warehouse expenses after the merger. Apparently Mr. Atkinson is a 'bottom line' guy so tell him that if he can give us twenty minutes, we can save him $2 million. Be specific."

Jeff smiled. "See Lorenzo, that's what makes her so good. She gets right to the heart of the problem."

Ortiz smiled. "I'm no salesman. You're right. If we say we can solve his biggest worry, he has to listen. But once I open the door, I'll let Sharon do the talking."

Jeff raised his glass to toast Sharon. Ortiz did not raise his. Both Sharon and Jeff looked at him.

"Sharon, as much as I'd like this deal to work—I can see your software saving my department thousands and thousands of dollars, and saving me personally many of my worst headaches—I wouldn't spend your commission check just yet."

"What's wrong?"

"Nothing's wrong. I just know Bill Atkinson. He spends money as though it is coming out of his own pocket. He's going to ask some very tough questions, and if he doesn't like the answers, you'll get nowhere with him. Once he starts fiddling with papers on his desk, I know whatever my request was, the answer is no. He has zero tolerance for hemming and hawing."

"Then maybe we should go over a list of questions you

think he's likely to ask so that we have ready answers."

Ortiz nodded.

"Grill me with anything," Sharon challenged.

"Okay. I think your price is way out of line. Justify it."

Jeff looked at Lorenzo. "I think making Sharon answer that is unfair."

"It's okay, Jeff. If Lorenzo thinks that's a question that Mr. Atkinson will really ask, then I'd better be prepared to answer it. Lots of salespeople would like to pretend their customers won't ask the tough questions. They will. I learned long ago to address the biggest concerns in the introduction so that they don't hang over my head and run around in the buyer's head the whole meeting, distracting them from everything we're trying to discuss."

"Good thinking," Lorenzo agreed as he watched Sharon jot notes.

Course Management

**In a complex sale, it is sometimes difficult to
clearly identify the key individuals who must "buy in"
to your solution. You will need to develop a relationship
strategy using your current supporters in order
to develop an effective plan.**

- On the customer's organizational chart, who is the key person with whom you must be aligned in order to win the business?
- Do you have an appealing statement of potential business value that will gain you access to key individuals?
- Do you know the political structure around the opportunity in order to implement the appropriate protocol and access the right people?
- Do you have an inside advocate who can provide this information and who will act on your behalf?

Sharon is confident she has a real solution for ToolTech.
Additionally, she has met the challenge of developing a plan that
will get her to the right people. Sharon knows the key individual
who must "buy in" to her ideas and she has made great success in
gaining the support of Lorenzo Ortiz, an individual who has direct
access to Bill Atkinson—the decision maker.

Sharon found that just as it is imperative to offer "compelling business
solutions" it is equally important to gain direct access with
senior level executives. Assembling an audience with the authority
to act upon your solutions is as vital as the solutions themselves.

Just as in Sharon's situation, salespeople must remember the importance of developing a strategy that is sensitive to the political
structure of an organization.

CHAPTER SIX

In trouble & scrambling

As Joan finished giving Sharon some details about the charity golf tournament over the phone, the younger woman apologized for yawning for at least the fifth time during the call.

"You sound tired," Joan said.

"I am," agreed Sharon. "I've been up pacing the floor every night this week."

"You lack 3 a.m. courage, eh?"

"Beg your pardon?"

"As I told you, my older brother is a bit of an amateur military historian. He told me a story—I have no idea if it's true or not—that Napoleon used to walk through his camp the night before a battle and see which of his officers were sleeping. After all the preparations were set, anyone who could be sound asleep at 3 a.m., was someone he thought he could trust to be cool and collected the next day. You do all you can; be as ready as you can, and then you go to bed."

"I guess I couldn't have cut it in Napoleon's army, either."

"It took me a long time to learn to ignore what I couldn't change at 3 a.m. I learned after a while, that most of what was keeping me up, I not only couldn't do anything about—at that hour anyway—but when looked at it in the light of day, wasn't really that big of a problem. So you have the jitters about the big presentation?"

"Well, that's part of it. I've never made a million-dollar sales pitch before. But that hasn't been my major worry."

"So what kept you awake all week?"

"My boss is ready to fire me, if he doesn't kill me first."

"What? I thought you're about to make the sale of a lifetime?"

"I am. I just may not live to see it. I've spent so much time researching Jeff's account, trying to woo him back, that I've let many of my smaller accounts slide."

"I don't know that much about your business, but you made it sound like Jeff *is* most of your business."

"He and maybe five other accounts are most of my business."

"How many other clients do you have?"

"Fifty or so."

"So if all of your business is with the five, does it really make sense to go on servicing the other accounts? I mean, did you ever stop to think what those other accounts cost you?'

"What do you mean, *cost me*? It's my job."

"But what does it cost? It's an old cliché, but 'time is money.' While you're out talking to the little guys, you're not selling Jeff's company. That costs something. Besides the lost opportunity with Jeff, have you ever figured out what a sales call costs you? Have you ever added up the phone calls, lunches, presentation materials, gas, the time and lost opportunity? Figure out what you make an hour and see what it costs you to make a call."

Sharon's head was spinning with the thought that she had never really looked at it from that point of view before. She was again amazed to find that she had just kept doing things the way she had been doing them without ever stopping to look at the *why* behind it. It was the problem they had discussed another day: A good golfer who hits a slump often has a harder time correcting it than a *great* golfer, who understands the mechanics of *how* things work.

"Have you ever tried to figure out," Joan began while Sharon's head was still reeling, "which is more cost-effective: one big sales call, several little ones, or hitting the panic button and starting to job hunt just when the deal is set?"

Sharon stared at her phone as though expecting it to answer Joan's question.

Joan waited a few moments and then said, "You've told me you were one of the top salespeople at your company. Did you get there by sitting around complaining that the male sales reps got all the good accounts?"

Since the question was obviously rhetorical, Sharon said nothing and let Joan continue.

"It's easy to be a victim. I know a woman who was an administrative assistant. She sat around bemoaning that she was stuck at the bottom due to the glass ceiling. Certainly lack of advancement for women is still a problem at some companies, but in the case of her company, it wasn't. Her boss was female. In fact, the CEO of the company was a woman. She found it less work to complain about the promotion than to do something for which someone might want to promote her. Taking the initiative requires work and courage."

Sharon listened intently as the older woman continued her lesson.

"It used to be enough to sit back and wait for your boss to tell you what to do. But, with the workload companies now demand from their employees as a matter of routine, that sort of passive approach is not going to get her promoted, and may not even keep her in her current job for very long. You can't wait for your boss to come to you. You need to go to her and tell her what needs to be done. And then do it."

Sharon smiled as she listened to Joan's voice through the receiver, nodding her head in silent agreement.

*   *   *   *   *   *   *   *   *   *   *   *

Sharon's first priority after talking to Joan had been to calculate what a sales call cost her. She dug out her records for the last ten years—her entire tenure at Software Solutions. She made a list of each of her clients and how much money each had made her. She went through her appointment books and added up how much time she had spent to make each of those sales. Between attending Max's soccer games over the weekend, she had crunched numbers, and Max had helped sort the list.

She was very surprised by what she had learned. Some of what she had regarded as good accounts had not earned her $1000 in commissions in the ten years she had worked with them. It was longevity and familiarity that made them seem important to her all out of proportion to their monetary worth. In some cases, she liked the client and spent time with them although they bought little. In other cases, the client was rather needy and demanded more attention. Because she had touched base with them almost once a week for years, they seemed a big part of her work life. Now, she could see, for the first time, what they really contributed to her paycheck.

ToolTech, on the other hand, had consistently accounted for 36-45 percent of her income for each year of her work with them. There was also that P.I.B. factor, as her former co-worker, Craig, liked to call it—'the pain-in-the-butt factor.' Some sales were just simpler and lower maintenance than others. Not only was ToolTech a good customer, Jeff Lee was easy to deal with. Other clients, whether they made money or not, were just annoying to be around.

Although it was difficult to quantify the P.I.B. factor, she could calculate a time-to-sale ratio, which would at least give her an idea which accounts made her enough in commissions to justify the work, regardless of the hassles.

She found it cost her $360 just to make a sales call. Considering how rarely some of her P.I.B. clients bought and what she had actually made from them, she quickly flagged about forty accounts on which she was actually losing money. The sales were so small that her cut was not even the $360 it cost her to call on them. And that certainly did not count what it cost her company. That had to run close to $1000, and it was hard to calculate the lost opportunity on top of that.

Sunday evening, after Max had gone to his room to do his

homework, she stared at her own homework and felt an odd emotion welling up in her—fear. What did all this information mean? That she was *never* to make another call on E.F. Striepeke & Co. or any of these other negative-net accounts again? She even wondered how she would fill her workweek if she stopped making half of her sales calls. Would she cease being so much of a salesperson and become more of a researcher, spending a week doing analysis and working out a business plan before she even approached the client? Would she find herself making 2 to 3 sales calls a week instead of 5 or 6 a day?

With a sudden stab of panic, Sharon grabbed her calendar. *All* of the next day's calls were on clients that she had just written off, starting with her rescheduled E.F. Striepeke meeting first thing in the morning. Was it possible that she could really take tomorrow off and actually save money?

Two hours later when Max came to tell her goodnight, she had crunched and re-crunched the numbers. Getting the same result as before, rather than reassuring her, just deepened her anxiety.

"Anything I can do, Mom?" Max asked earnestly, when he saw the troubled look on her face.

"No, Honey," she said, hugging him goodnight. "I'm just still trying to sort out some things for work." She couldn't tell him that she was suddenly completely confused by what she did for a living. That she had just realized that for the last ten years she had been doing her job all wrong.

"If you want to leave me a list of stuff to do when I get home from soccer tomorrow...."

She hugged him harder. "I wish I knew what either of us was supposed to do tomorrow."

Sharon stayed up late that night sorting and sifting. She wished she had paid more attention in her economics classes. She had grasped all of those principles long enough to take the test and then let them slip into a haze since they did not seem that relevant in her life. She struggled to recall things like Pareto's Law: the 80-20 rule. That 20 percent of your customers created 80 percent of your bottom line. If she had applied that ten years ago, she thought, she would not have spent 80 percent of her time pursuing 20 percent of her income.

She remembered the real estate agent who had sold her this house telling her that he had dumped two-thirds of his listings and had tripled his commissions. Now she finally understood how that could be. By concentrating his energies on the sales he was most likely to make, he did not spread himself too thin and could make each of the sales he did make, faster.

In her frustration and confusion, she kicked herself for not being a better student and paying more attention to those seemingly contradictory ideas of how you could have a cash flow, but not be making money, or how you could save money by not having one. Cash flow and other tricky little accounting things made it hard to see the bottom line. If she had just figured her cost and income, it would have made life so much simpler. If she kept those five appointments tomorrow, she knew she would most likely make one sale. Possibly two. They would create income, but would they make money?

She went to bed, but woke at 3 a.m., and, after trying unsuccessfully to get back to sleep, got up to stare at her figures some more. She decided to try a different approach. She reduced each client to an index card and tried sorting them every which way she could: by the type of business, size of company, the amount of business she did with them, the length of time she had serviced the account, whether her sales with them were rising or falling, whether the client's company was growing or shrinking, even whether or not she liked the contact person she dealt with at the company.

She then tried to combine and quantify these divisions. About the time she woke Max for school, she was beginning to see a pattern. The 80-20 rule really did apply. ToolTech and seven other companies accounted for 84 percent of her sales.

And ToolTech was half of that. All five of the calls she intended to make today had, in their history, brought less than 2 percent of her business.

Being unsure what to do otherwise, however, she showered and went to her first appointment.

While waiting in the outer office of E.F. Striepeke, Sharon questioned why she was even there. When she asked herself why had she not canceled today's calls she realized it boiled down to one thing: Fear. She was afraid *not* to be there. She was afraid of not knowing what to do if she were not there.

She remembered Joan saying that fear was a great motivator. What usually prompts a person to change, Joan had said, was when the fear of what will happen if we continue to do things the way we have always done them becomes greater than the fear of the unknown of what will happen if we make changes. It is what caused people to jump from burning buildings—the fear of the flames becomes greater than the fear of the jump.

Sharon had to admit that at this point she was very afraid of what it meant if she did not go through with today's meetings. She was afraid to tell these accounts that they simply were not worth servicing any longer. She was afraid to tell her boss, Alan Miller, that she wanted to junk most of her accounts. She could just picture the look on Alan's face. And what was the alternative? Put all of her eggs in the ToolTech basket? Spend all of her time trying to find a way to make that one sale? And what if she failed? She would have no accounts, big or small, and certainly no job.

Clearly she had to go on making the small sales until she sold ToolTech and the other large clients on her list. She had just started making notes to herself of things to learn about her own company and her other clients when the secretary told her she could go in.

In what Sharon had started referring to as 'the good old days'—but were really less than two years ago—she would have counted on making three or four out of five sales calls. Today she would have been extremely happy to make two, but was quite satisfied with the one order she did get.

What had changed in those two years? Was it, as she and Joan had discussed, that the Internet/information age had really fully arrived? As Joan noted, although most people are not yet to the point that they buy their cars or houses on the web, they may do their homework on the web and price comparison shop before they ever leave the house to make that major a purchase. Joan said she looked up the amount the dealer paid for her car before she went to the dealership. And, armed with that information, her negotiations took on a whole new angle.

Sharon called Max before her last appointment and asked him to start looking up a few things on the web. She also promised to pick up pizza on the way home. Not only was it his favorite meal, she knew it would be easy to eat in front of the computer.

There was a lot more she wanted to learn about her other clients before she was willing to jettison her smaller accounts.

*   *   *   *   *   *   *   *   *   *   *   *

Sharon worked hard all week trying to keep up with her smaller accounts, while still trying to make sure things were on track for getting her R & D people to talk to several individuals at ToolTech. She knew she was not doing her usual thorough job with her other clients, but she could not find enough time to do both. By the time she met Joan for her weekly golf game, she had tons of information about all of her clients. Most of it was not good.

"Joan, one of these days, you're going to tell me to quit whining and go home."

"Uh oh. What happened this week?"

"Are you sure you want to hear?"

"In for a penny, in for a pound. I've come this far. I have to see how the next chapter comes out."

"You may be sorry. I'm not sure this book has a happy ending."

"So, you didn't get to see the elusive VP at Jeff's company?"

"Are you kidding? We saw him. He loved the pitch. Things are going great! He apologized for being so hard to reach, but said that he's been given the assignment of making this merger cost-effective. He had given strict orders not to be disturbed by anyone who couldn't make that happen. He's thrilled I've finally given him the cost savings he needed to make it work. I've provided him with a value that no one else can touch!"

"Attagirl!" Joan cheered.

"It was great. Once we got the meeting, Ortiz, who was so nervous going in, suddenly would not shut up. He was so excited about how much money our software would save his department, how much easier his job would be, and how it would simplify the melding of the departments after the merger. He was so gung-ho on it, he got the VP all fired-up about it that—I hardly had to say a word. He is the best salesperson I could've asked for. And, since he works for them, it doesn't look like I'm trying to sell them something. In the few meetings we've had so far, Erick and I—Erick is one of our engineers—just went along for the ride and to answer a few questions. It was pretty funny, actually, the first time I let Erick near Jeff's company. You get some of these engineers out from behind their computers, and let them talk to someone and they'll spew out a long laundry list of things the product can do—"

"Data dumping?" Joan asked laughingly as she interrupted. Sharon smiled. "I learned that from you," Joan teased.

"I'm glad I could finally teach you something."

"Oh, I've learned a lot more than that from you, Sharon."

"Thanks."

"The thing is while you are doing that, *data dumping*, you aren't really listening to the customer, right?"

"Exactly. In this case, Ortiz was so wired about the idea, that I wanted him to do most of the talking. You know the old adage, *'People love to buy, they just hate to be sold.'* I was more than happy to let him explain, rather than me sell. I loved having him there to carry the ball."

The starter signaled them, and they walked toward the tee.

"That's great! How is that bad news?"

"I may not have a job to reap the rewards."

"What? Your boss still can't want to fire you?"

"I still haven't *sold* anything. And Alan has lost faith in my predictions of sales to come. Like the boy who cried wolf, I've had this sale to Jeff on my list forever and still haven't made the sale. If I put it on my forecast for next quarter—and up the sale to what it'll be—$2 million, my boss is never going to believe it. He'll just think I've gone crazy and fire me right then and there."

"He can't wait a little while longer, to see how this comes out?"

"I'm not sure he can. His numbers for the whole department are so low, he may not have much time himself. His boss, Estelle Washington, is on him constantly now. She's under a ton of pressure herself. Companies have become so immediate-results-oriented, that the average sales VP stays in their job for only two years. Some people at work think she has already overstayed her welcome. She budgeted a 15 percent *increase* in sales this year. Where she came up with that one, I have no idea. Certainly not with any input from anyone in our department. Right now we're looking at a 40 percent *decrease*—at least."

"Unless you can sell Jeff."

"Right."

"Which means buying time with Alan," Joan suggested.

"Which I'm not sure I can. I guess it's partially my fault. Maybe mainly my fault. I was so concerned about what went on outside the company—keeping my clients happy—that I never took the time to get to know Alan or most of my fellow employees, or their problems. I spent so little time in the office that now—when I need to take an interest—it may be too late.

"Like the million-dollar star of a sports team, when things are going good, you reap the rewards, but when things go bad, the star gets blamed first and most. I almost get the feeling Alan is going to pink-slip me out of spite. Execute the ring-leader as a lesson to the others—you know the old *'firings-will-continue-until-moral-improves'* school of management. It'll show Estelle he's serious about making changes. I think he has always resented that I make more money than he does. Like the coach who's making half of what his players are making, he feels they're a little ungovernable because of it.

"To make matters worse, I'm not sure most of my fellow reps aren't enjoying my fall from grace. The only one I took the time to get to know, Craig, is long gone, and I may soon be joining him."

"How much time do you think you have left?"

"Probably not much. The quarter ends next week. And if I have nothing—and I'll still have nothing by then—I think I'm gone."

"When you're this close, though, he has to give you more time, doesn't he?"

"Does he? Estelle Washington is the *'or-heads-will-roll'* type. She's desperate, so he's desperate, so I'm desperate. Sort of the trickle-down effect. I think Alan's thinking it's my head or his. If he gets rid of me, it'll prove to Estelle he's doing all he can, and I think he thinks it'll scare everyone else into pro-ducing. If he's willing to fire his star, they'll all know their jobs are also hanging by a thread, and do something. What they will do except continue to run in circles, I don't know. As far as I know, at least from what Alan has said, I'm the only one who has chosen to slack off on my smaller accounts. They're all still doing everything they can—running themselves to death. In one case I really fear it'll happen. One of my fellow reps, Keith, is sixty, overweight, smokes, and if this kind of pressure keeps up, he can't last long. They're all working eighty-hour weeks to make sales, any sales, no matter how small, just to have money coming in for Alan."

"Even though it's costing them money?" Joan asked.

"Yes, even though it's costing them money," Sharon agreed. "The real problem, as I've discovered, isn't with the reps. It's that the business has changed, and we can't keep trying to compete on product, service, and price when the product and service are so similar and these little companies can undercut us on price. Doing business the old way, the sales just aren't there. I know our only hope is to change the game and do business a new way. I think my way will work, but I have to get Alan to see that."

Sharon paused for a breath and a heavy sigh. Joan gave her shoulder a reassuring pat.

"I'm ranting. I'm sorry."

"It's okay. I understand. You have reason to."

The women both hit their drives and started down the fairway after their balls. Joan pointed at the weeds. "I see our bunny friend is back."

"With his little friends," Sharon tried to smile at the cute little faces twitching their noses as they munched grass. Not much of a smile found its way to her lips. She realized she should be enjoying such a beautiful day on the course with Joan, surrounded by nature. She realized she needed to start enjoying life more, but now the thought that she didn't even have the time for that made her even more tense.

"A rabbit's foot is supposed to be good luck, and I count about twenty-eight over there. So lets take this as a good omen. Are you sure you can't get Alan to listen to reason?"

"I don't know, Joan. I tried to talk to him early on about

SSI's goals, but he blew me off. Then, after that reaction, I wanted to make sure everything was in place with the R & D people, the engineers, and everything, *before* I talked to him again. First, I wanted to be sure that the engineers could do what was needed and that Jeff's company was interested. Otherwise, Alan would have thought I was crazy to suggest I stop selling software and start selling a new business partnership with our clients. I guess it was a mistake ducking him for so long. I think I waited *too* long."

"Don't think of them as mistakes. I like to think of those as times when I learned something different from what I set out to learn. Edison supposedly once said something like, '*I have not failed. I have just discovered over 10,000 things that make lousy light bulb filaments.*'"

"That's an awfully optimistic way of looking at things. You know, there's a momentum to every relationship—personal as well as business. A moment when the time is right. I'm afraid I may have missed that moment with Alan. And if I take much longer getting things rolling with Jeff's company, I may miss the opportunity there as well."

"Sounds like you need a stay of execution."

"Yes, but I don't think the governor's call will come in time to save me."

"So call him."

"I can't...."

"Yes, you can. You found the courage to see the VP and make him listen. You've certainly got what it takes to see your own boss. Beg if you have to. Don't let your ego get in the way of clear judgment." They both played irons to the green. "Apologize to Alan and ask for more time."

"I really haven't done anything to apologize for. I was just doing my job, the best way I knew how...."

"Ego, Sharon. Apologize anyway. You said you feel bad about the way things have worked out. So apologize. You'll both feel better. Get him alone and talk to him. *Really* talk to him. Not these short little one-sentence exchanges you tell me you keep having. A conversation. He's running scared. You said so yourself, and fear clouds the judgment as much as ego. Get him alone, explain the situation and give him time to think rationally."

"Alan is under so much pressure to do something, he may not have the time to give, even if—"

"You're already deciding how this'll come out? How do you know unless you ask? You surely have failed if you don't even *ask*. And another thing, you *are* doing something. If you can show him you have a $2 million deal in the works with Jeff, he has to let you see it through. Get Jeff to call him if you have to. Or Jeff's boss. Or the transportation guy. Or the invisible VP. But find a way to prove to Alan you are working. Not only working, but working on a deal that will make you and him and your company, money. If Alan won't listen, then talk to Estelle, and if she won't listen, talk to her boss. This deal is too important to let Alan kill it."

"I can't do that. I'm way too low in the pecking order."

"You're letting fear cloud your judgment, just like Alan. You were just as low when you were selling with the mystery vice-president who never sees anyone. You saw him, and you sold him. If you want to, you can."

"That was different. I was consulting to their company. I was the outside expert with the answers. At my company, I'm just a peon. No one has to listen to me."

"But you're a peon with the answers, and if anyone at the company on any level, rung-by-rung above you, has any brains they will listen to you. You had to sell Jeff's company rung-by-rung; now you have to take the time and make the effort to sell your own company the same way. Sales is sales, Sharon, inside your company, or outside. You've told me you are good at what you do. Prove it."

"I'm just one woman in a huge organization, why should anyone take me seriously."

After they putted, Joan fixed Sharon with a hard look.

"You mean one woman can't make a difference? What can one woman do? Ask Rosa Parks. It wasn't some grand committee that decided to end discrimination. It was one woman. Ask Candy Lightner what a woman can do. It wasn't a thousand law makers who changed the way we look at drinking and driving, it was one woman who was determined, and founded Mothers Against Drunk Driving. Ask Rachel Carson what a woman can do. Before she wrote *Silent Spring* no one in government or industry gave any thought to environmental protection.

"Now I'm not suggesting that your calling is as important, or as earth-shattering and as capable of changing society, but think how much easier it is to change one little company than to change the world. Your idea may not be as big as those, but it just goes to show you what one determined person with a good idea can do. And you will find, I am sure, as those women did, that once the idea catches on, there will be no shortage of allies. My brother likes to quote Victor Hugo, '*The invasion of armies can be resisted, but not an idea whose time has come.*'"

"I see your point, but I'm just one woman with an idea that my boss has already called crazy."

"You just said he's hardly listened to any of it. Once he hears the entire idea, I think that will change." Joan paused and changed the subject as they walked to the next hole.

"Speaking of women being able to do anything they want, can I tell you a cute story?"

"Sure."

"My three-year-old granddaughter, Michelle, was visiting me. I had arranged for her to play with the little girl who lives next to me, Sara. Michelle came home all upset, on the verge of tears. I asked what was wrong, and she said she and Sara were playing and that Sara's father told Michelle she couldn't be what she wanted when she grew up. Well, I got all indignant. I told her she most certainly could grow up to be whatever she wanted, and she should never settle for less than that, and she should never let anyone tell her different. I was just about to go next door and give Sara's father a piece of my mind, but I first wanted to get the facts straight so I asked, 'Sara, tell me. What is it you want to be when you grow up, dear?' and she said, 'A basset hound like Sara has.'"

Sharon and Joan both laughed. "So I guess there is also a moral here about how important it is to be in full possession of the facts," Joan concluded when they were done laughing.

After their drives, as they walked off the tee, Joan asked, "Did you know that 60 percent of new businesses are started by women?"

"Really?"

"And, I've read that although most new businesses still fail, those started by women have a higher success rate than those started by men?"

"Is that true?" Sharon asked, not doubting Joan's word, but just reconfirming Joan's statement. "Why do you suppose that is?"

"I don't know. Maybe we're just more tenacious." Joan smiled. "The little graph I saw offered no explanations."

"Maybe women just try harder and have to be more innovative, just to compete. But I just don't know if anyone in the company will take my suggestions coming from so far below."

"They all have to know something is seriously wrong, and if you offer a solution to the crisis, do you think anyone is going to care from how far down it came? Do you think a man in a burning building is going to tell the firefighters to take their ladder and go away—that he wants to be rescued by no one less than the chief? They have to know they need help, and if they are smart, they'll accept it from whatever direction it comes."

Sharon stared thoughtfully at her driver as Joan continued. "I was organizing a charity function once, and while I was on the phone, laying out this big complicated plan, the man was there fixing the cable TV. The whole time I was talking he was chuckling. The park where we were to hold our art fair had booked a children's fair the day before. So instead of having all day Saturday to set up, the park would be in use. The company from whom we had rented our tents and tables and chairs was going to have to stay up all night getting ready. It was going to cost us a fortune in double-time, eliminating most of the proceeds that were to go to charity.

"I was livid that this man could laugh at my predicament, and I demanded to know what was so funny. And he said, 'You, lady. You could just contact the children's fair people, ask what kind of tents they are using, and ask to rent theirs.' I could've stayed angry, but instead, I just laughed and agreed I was being stupid, complicating things unnecessarily. I could have dismissed the idea since it only came from the cable guy and not someone 'important' like the senator's wife I had been talking to, or I could thank him for saving us a lot of work. He saved us work, the children's fair people work, and a lot of money, too. We rented one set of tents for two days, at far less than half the cost we would have each paid individually."

Sharon shook her head, "I just finished taking on Jeff's whole company, I'm not sure I can take on mine."

"You don't have to. You just have to talk with one person at a time."

Joan pulled out her 3-wood and removed its stocking.

"I tried to tell Alan that most of my accounts aren't worth my time anymore, and tried to tell him that many don't really make the company money, either. But he just can't see it that way. He can't understand how losing an account—any account—no matter how small—can be good business."

"You have honors," Joan said.

"I'm sorry, Joan, I got so wound up there, I forgot we're supposed to be playing golf. No, you go ahead."

Joan hit her usual consistent shot, and Sharon topped hers

sending it straight, but barely a hundred yards. A bunny ducked for cover.

"Those little guys are going to start hating me," Sharon said.

"The hazards of life on the fairway, I guess," Joan smiled. "But we all have our own perspectives, and have a hard time seeing things from anyone else's. That's what ruins a lot of relationships, including a lot of marriages. We assume everyone else has the same idea we do. Do you think that bunny cares that you're probably going to bogey this hole?"

"No, his problem is that I almost hit him with a ball," Sharon answered, as though the rabbit could hear her apology.

"So your trivial goal of par means nothing to him given how much bigger his problem is from his point of view."

As they walked off the tee, Joan said, "You said you understand why Alan is upset. Do you also understand what is keeping *him* awake at night? He has problems, too."

Sharon studied her mentor for a hint of what was coming next.

"Really try to see it from his point of view. You understand the easy part—your sales shrink, your income shrinks, which shrinks the sales that Alan's department has produced, which shrinks the gross his department has produced."

"Right. As I said, I appreciate his problem—"

"The part that's your problem. Not the other half of his world, which is why he can't see that it's a waste of time for you to continue calling on smaller accounts."

Sharon hit her next shot as she pondered this. It did not go far, either.

As Sharon replaced the club in her bag, Joan asked, "How is Alan's performance measured?"

"By the gross his sales team produces."

"And that gross is shrinking," acknowledged Joan. "Certainly can't blame him for wanting every dollar he can get to add to that total."

"But it's costing us money."

"Until recently, did you see things that way? Why should he?"

"Good point," agreed Sharon.

"And he may not care what it costs *you* to make a sale, but he may stop and think if you can show him how much those little accounts cost the company. Get him to see the big picture. See how that fits, or doesn't fit, in with your company's overall goals and strategies. Maybe he is as unaware of your company's goals as you were until you started digging."

"You're right. I'm sure he is trapped in the same tunnel vision I was. As long as his sales department was making money, there was no reason he should look around at *how* it was making it."

"Bingo! People do that all the time. Focus on the one little thing they understand—their own point of view. They forget the big picture and the overall objective. I did that with the charity art thing. Got so busy being little Ms. Organization, all wrapped up in details, that I forgot the event wasn't about me and my ability to take charge, or even the tents—it was to raise money for a good cause."

"You found the key point that got the door open to that VP. You know what keeps Alan awake at night. Address that issue, and I bet he'll listen. And if not, ask yourself what is keeping the president of your company awake. He or she will listen."

"This may just work out yet."

"It will. Now may I putt?"

Sharon dramatically bowed her head in respectful silence as Joan putted her ball into the hole—for a twelve-foot birdie. Sharon then 3-putted to complete her butchered hole.

Joan smiled. "Can I share one other thing I have learned?"

"Please."

"When you find the right solution, you'll often find it's not just a win-win, but a win-win-win. Both the children's fair and my charity made more money, but in the process we made *less* work, not more work, for ourselves. If the answer is right, it often works better for everyone. In your case, if your idea works right, you'll not only make more money, but you can make yourself, and your boss look better in the process. Jeff will get kudos, and his company will make more money. But in the process you are saving a lot of paperwork flying back and forth, saving extra cartons and extra shipping, so it even works better for the environment and everyone wins."

"Let's just hope Alan can see all that 'winning.'"

As they walked to the next tee, Joan asked, "You said you'd started looking at your other accounts, right? Using the same framework you developed for Jeff, you should be able to sell at least some of your other large clients, right?"

"And I still can't picture myself telling Alan we're just going to stop selling 90 percent of my clients."

"Maybe you just need to find a more cost-effective way to handle them."

Sharon wondered if it was because she was so tired or because her brain was full, that once again Joan had puzzled her.

Sharon yelled "Fore!" to send a bunny scurrying off the fairway before she teed up her ball.

EXECUTIVE SUMMARY

In Trouble and Scrambling

As you move into the "sales consultant" role, you will undoubtedly encounter various obstacles that you must be able and willing to face in order to be successful.

- As a salesperson, do you understand that less is more?
- Do you realize that spending time focusing on the 20 percent of your clients who are high potential would actually be more effective than servicing all of them?
- Are you prepared to help your company create more effective ways to service different types of customers?
- Do you understand the "big picture" of management within your own sales organization?

Sharon is discovering the importance of Pareto's Law—something members of direct sales forces need to remember. Knowing who the top 20 percent of your clients are brings a focus and efficiency to any sales organization.

This narrowed focus results in the creation of several ways in which clients may be serviced. As it stands today, most sales organizations are struggling today to make it easy for customers to do business with them. Traditionally, most sales were generated by a direct sales force. Yet, in today's market, as salespeople become "sales consultants," companies will have to re-engineer their sales methods to include an e-commerce approach.

Through her own research, Sharon has created a plan that will be a "win-win-win" situation for all in involved. Now, she has to muster the courage to buck the system. Just as she had to understand the big picture for ToolTech, she must now understand the big picture of those within her own company.

CHAPTER SEVEN

Getting aligned

Saturday morning Sharon found herself back at the golf course, anxiously watching for Alan's car. She had come close to begging to get him out of the office—and away from his ever-ringing phone, with its crisis of the moment—and away from all the distractions, to try to really talk to him. She had explained that she knew things were not good, and she wanted one last chance to explain. After all the years she had made his department so much money, couldn't he grant her nine holes of golf?

But Alan was late. Not a good sign, Sharon thought. If he were as eager for this meeting as she was, he would have been early. Sharon always planned to be early for her appointments—it was one of the things that made her so good at her job. Normally, if she arrived early, she would do paperwork in her car. Now, she was too nervous to even think about paperwork.

Alan had seemed so hesitant to even agree to meet, and his being late seemed to reinforce her idea that he was not going to be a very receptive audience. As she waited, she realized she was not sure how to talk with him. She had never *really* talked with him. They had not been unfriendly, but their transactions had been all business and to the point. She was not even sure how to play it with him—friendly and chatty, or all business and direct. She wished she had researched him as thoroughly as she would have any client.

To prepare for this meeting with Alan, Sharon once again turned to the Internet for research. This time, instead of researching a client, she researched her own company, Software Solutions, Inc. She came across old annual reports and organizational charts. With Max's help, she assembled a detailed picture of the company for which she had worked for nearly a decade, and now was realizing she barely knew.

With her research complete, she knew the company inside and out. What she did not know, and had not thought to look at, was Alan. He seemed so familiar since she had known him for ten years, but she had known him on such a superficial level that now that it mattered, she realized she did not know him at all.

Finally Alan's car wheeled into the lot. He got out more with the movements of one about to serve as pallbearer at a friend's funeral than those of a man about to play a game.

Sharon took a deep breath and used it to force a smile to her lips. She strode to his car with as much of a bounce in her step as she could muster.

"Good morning, Alan."

"Is it?" he asked with such coldness that she began to wonder if he would fire her before the first tee.

Sharon took another breath. "I think so. It's a beautiful morning, a great day for golf. We're away from the stress of the office. We have a great golf course, an awesome view...."

Sharon was not sure if there was a word buried in Alan's grunted reply or not. Whatever it was, it was certainly not a seconding of her sentiments.

While Alan laced his spikes, Sharon went to the booth and learned from the starter that because they had missed their tee time by more than thirty minutes, he would have to try to squeeze them in whenever. That would take at least an hour.

Sharon took a moment to decide how to present this to Alan. With the foul mood he was in, she did not want to make it sound as though she were blaming him for the missed time. She took another breath and then re-crossed the parking lot, her soft spikes squeaking on the asphalt. Alan sat on his car's bumper, cursing at his shoelace.

"No hurry," she said in as chipper a voice as possible. "There is some mix up on the tee time. We'll have to wait a bit.

"Swell," Alan said, "You know I didn't think this golf game was such a good idea, anyway."

"I'm sorry, I just thought—"

"Thought what, Sharon? That if you took me golfing it would somehow change your sales figures?"

"No, of course not, Alan. I just hoped it would give us time away from the office to finally talk."

"A little late for talk, isn't it? You've wanted to do your own thing for so long—like some kind of gunslinger—and now that things are going bad, you finally want me to make time to talk to you."

"Alan, let's be honest. You didn't really want to talk to me, either. And realistically, as long as my numbers were good, and, by extension, yours were good, there really wasn't much reason for us to talk."

Alan opened his mouth to protest, but Sharon kept talking to finish her point. "I'm willing to admit now, that I was wrong. I shouldn't have seen it as us just getting in each other's way, but rather I should've been looking for a way for us to work together to improve the overall output. I don't think it's too late for us to start doing that now."

Again Alan opened his mouth to say something, then closed it again, letting Sharon continue.

"I'd like to tell you what I have been up to...."

Suddenly Alan could no longer hold his tongue, "I've heard what you've been up to. More of your lone escapades, trying to take over engineering—"

"Not take over, work with," Sharon protested, immediately sorry she had let such a defensive and angry tone creep in. But it was hard not to meet Alan's anger with equal venom. Sharon took another deep breath and sat down quietly on the bumper of his car.

"I'm sorry, Alan. I know I should've talked to you first. That was wrong. But we've never talked much, and I didn't want to tell you about it until I was sure it'd work."

"Do you know how stupid I felt getting a phone call from Vicky Fong and having no idea what she was talking about? Like I don't know what my own sales department is up to?" His loud angry tone sent one of the course's many rabbits running for cover. Sharon wished she could join the little bunny, wherever he was, ducking to hide.

"I'm sorry. I wasn't even sure what I was looking for when I went poking around down in engineering. I would've felt dumb enough if I had come up with nothing, let alone if I had dragged you into it."

"As far as I can see, it's just more of your playing Lone Ranger and wasting time doing it."

"When I tried to tell you about my Internet research and ask you about SSI's goals, you kind of saw it that way. That's another reason I didn't want to tell you about engineering until I was sure I had something."

"You mean until you were sure you got all of the credit."

"Not at all, Alan. I want you to go with me to Ms. Washington. I'd like you to meet with Vicky and Erick from engineering, and then for all of us go to Ms. Washington and tell her what we're proposing—some changes we think need to be made. Some rather big changes."

"What are you talking about, Sharon? SSI just made some major changes last year. They redesigned the logo, came up with a new slogan, started using just SSI instead of the full *Software Solutions, Inc.* in advertising, changed everyone's job title...."

"Alan, it's going to take a lot more than new business cards to change the slump this company is in."

"The company isn't in a slump. You are. You and the rest of the reps who have gotten so complacent they hardly bother making sales calls any more!"

"We're not doing anything any differently. In fact, the rest of the reps are all working harder than they ever have before."

"I'm sure not seeing the results."

"Because the world has changed. And we need to change with it. Change ahead of it, if we can."

"We will. When 5.0 comes out in a few months it'll be the best thing on the market—"

"Alan, it was supposed to be out last year! So, at best, it's little better than last year's technology. And we will be lucky if it comes out by the *end* of this year."

"And when it does come out, we'll regain all the market share we lost and then some!"

"Do you really think Ms. Washington is going to wait that long to see results?"

For the first time Alan paused, and Sharon realized she had scored a point.

"Remember, she predicted a sales *increase*. If she doesn't come up with that, who do you think she'll blame?"

Alan was stunned for another moment, like a boxer blind-sided by a right hook. But he quickly shook it off, and said defensively, "SSI will bounce back. It always has."

"I'm sure the makers of LaSalle, and Hudson, and a few dozen other now-extinct automakers, thought that, too. Not to mention Builder's Emporium. Bigger companies than ours have made the *it'll bounce back* mistake."

"That's different."

"Is it? The railroads failed to grasp they were in the *transportation* business, not the *people-moving* business, and tried to compete head-to-head with the airlines. It didn't work. We can't pretend the world is the same. Like the Polish cavalry attacking tanks with swords."

"What?"

"In 1939, when Germany invaded Poland, the Polish cavalry tried to stop the panzers with brave, but obviously useless, saber charges." Then, to justify her analogy, Sharon continued, "A friend of mine is sort of into military history. She's famous for using military analogies. I borrowed that one from her."

Alan shook his head as though confirming to himself that

Sharon had gone crazy.

Sharon decided to try a different way. "Did you know Reese is letting their entire sales force go?"

Again Alan looked like a fighter who had just had his bell rung. "Where did you hear that?"

"I've been trying to tell you, I've done a lot of research, not only on ToolTech and SSI, but on our competition as well. Reese can no longer afford to pay their reps. None of their reps were making enough to cover their draws. They kept scaling back and scaling back.... Does this sound familiar?"

Alan's face puckered. "What're they going to do?"

"Just take phone orders."

"Well, that won't happen to us. When 5.0 comes out—"

"We said that about 4.0."

"And when it came out, sales jumped 40 percent—"

"And then flat-lined six months later when Reese pulled their little valu-price stunt. All of our products are so similar, and differentiation has become so elusive, that we can at best tread water. We get these little momentary movements forward or backward that, when you look at the big picture over the last ten years, mean nothing. We have almost exactly the same average market share year after year. So do LatCo and Reese."

"But, when 5.0 comes out—"

"Stop it, Alan. It'll be a little blip on the big chart. That's all. I made all these same arguments to myself, and to my golf buddy, Joan. She said the way I clung to false hope was the way they talk about Hitler. As Berlin was falling, he exhorted the German people to fight on a little longer—new wonder weapons would save the day. Alan, 5.0 is no 'wonder weapon.' Have you seen it? What it's going to do?"

"It's going to be twice as fast as 4.0, and—"

"It is a marginal difference at best. While I'd rather describe it in an unladylike manner, I'll just stick with polite terms."

"Sharon, I can't believe you're talking this way about the best products SSI has to offer!"

"And our best simply isn't good enough to ever really get ahead. It's barely good enough to compete. We've been losing ground in this rat race for a long time. The rats are burnt out, and there's no finish line in sight. If we don't make some serious changes in the way we do business, you could find yourself supervising an order-entry department. But somehow I doubt you'll stick around to do that, or that Ms. Washington will go on paying you what they pay you, just to run a phone staff."

Stunned into silence, Alan sat quietly as Sharon laid out the new software proposal that she had worked out with engineering, Jeff and ToolTech. Alan stayed silent as she detailed how well the plan had gone over not only with Jeff, but the head of transportation, and all the way up to the VP of operations. The next step was the president of ToolTech.

Sharon was getting stiff sitting on the bumper, but as long as Alan was listening attentively, she didn't want to shift position and give him an opportunity to interrupt.

She realized how badly she was misreading Alan when, just as she was about to wrap up her explanation, Alan suddenly stood up, still with one shoe off. She thought he had been following her outline and understanding what all this meant, when he burst forth with, "This is what you have been spending all your time doing?"

"Yes, I—"

"How many weeks just to try to sell one client? No wonder I've been getting calls from other companies wondering where the hell you've been, and why you haven't returned their calls."

Sharon thought about correcting him, but Alan had so much anger and frustration that he wanted to vent, that until he did, he would be unlikely to listen to reason. She just sat and nodded as he criticized her about how poor her and the rest of the sales department's figures were.

Each time he raised his voice, golfers around the parking lot looked over. Sharon tried to keep a calm enough face so that no one would think anything was really wrong, while at the same time making Alan know she was listening and taking him seriously. Like an over-inflated balloon, he needed to let go of some of the pressure before he exploded. Alan paused a few times as though expecting Sharon to rebut or argue, but instead she just nodded sympathetically. Finally he had spent all of his pent-up frustration and stopped talking.

Sharon stood up. "I understand you're upset. And, I'm sorry I didn't communicate more effectively. I also know you're under a lot of pressure to hit the numbers. I've been experiencing similar pressure about my own performance. I went through a lot of this same anger and confusion. Now I feel really bad that we weren't more help to each other since we're going through the same thing. Alan may I ask who you have talked to about this problem?"

Sharon struggled to keep her cool and not *leap* into an argument, which was very tempting to do when confronted with such bull-headed hostility. It was a good way of handling not only clients but people in general. She often turned to that simple technique when dealing with her son. She had to really hear and understand Alan's point of view, before he would be willing to listen to hers and together they could forge a solution.

Alan was not making this process easy. "Talked to?" he barked. "I don't need to talk to anyone. I can read sales reports!"

"You seem to be under a lot of pressure to hit the numbers," Sharon empathized.

"That's an understatement."

"So you're not aware of any particular problems any of the reps are having?"

"I'm aware that they are not making sales, and from some

of the calls I've received from your customers, I can understand why."

"Actually, Alan, I'm the only one who has been reducing the number of sales calls I make. I've spoken to the other reps, and they're working harder than they ever have and the sales simply aren't out there. Do you know how many more hours and how many more calls they're all making? Customers simply are not buying. When was the last time all of the reps actually made quota?"

Alan shrugged, annoyed. "At least a couple of years."

"Have you asked them, or even yourself, why that might be?"

"I think you've all just gotten too complacent."

"But have you asked the reps, or any of our customers, what they think is wrong?"

Alan snorted.

Sharon continued. "I know we've not always communicated well, but I think we can help each other now."

"A bit late for that."

"I have had some of my little accounts slide, but—"

"You have no *little* accounts, Sharon. Each and every one of them means important business to SSI."

"I hate to contradict you, Alan, but the fact is that some of my accounts are much more important than others to SSI. This ToolTech deal, for instance, is going to be worth about $2 million. E.F. Striepeke's entire company is not worth that."

Alan was already poised to say something when what Sharon had said caught him by surprise and he stopped. "How much?" he asked, in a much different tone.

"Two...million...dollars." Sharon drew out each word for emphasis.

Sharon knew she had not planned this talk with Alan well at all. If she had, she would have known to use that number to get his attention first. She had not given enough time to advance preparation, and had let Alan's tardiness and anger—

and her own nervousness—spoil any clear thought process she usually was able to follow during a presentation. Sharon realized that she was doing all the talking and wondered why listening was so much more difficult to do when selling her boss than selling to clients.

Luckily this *sale* to Alan had not yet completely fallen apart and now that she finally had his attention, she had better use it.

"Think about it. We're going to be selling software to each of ToolTech's divisions. Not just Jeff's one area. And not only to ToolTech, but the new, much larger ToolTech that will be created when they merge with CTC."

"ToolTech is merging with CTC? Where did you hear that?"

"As I told you, I've been doing a lot of research."

"Hmmm."

"And get this, that two-million dollar figure doesn't include the software we'll be selling to all of ToolTech's suppliers. If their vendors want to stay on ToolTech's favored list, they'll have to buy our software to integrate with the system. All the companies with which they do business will have to have our software to link up to their new system—right down to the trucking companies that do their shipping. Instead of just selling a product, we can address their critical business problems. I look at it as emphasizing the second part of our name: *Solutions* instead of just *Software*."

Sharon now knew she had Alan hooked, so she went on, "And think about how this changes our relationship with them from just being a supplier to being far more of a strategic business partner. We'll be their single-source supplier. They won't run back to LatCo or Reese if one of those companies drops its price a few dollars. It isn't changing software at this point, it would be changing systems, and that would take so much money and effort that they will be very reluctant to do it...."

"So every time the competition makes a little move we

won't lose 80 percent of market share, only to get it back when we make some little change," Alan said, completing her thought.

"Exactly. We're no longer just a product. We're their partner."

"Let me see this plan!"

Sharon trotted across the parking lot to her car. By the time she had her car trunk open and her briefcase in her hands, Alan was standing next to her, still with one golf shoe on and one off. Alan tore into the file like a kid into a birthday gift. Alan stopped at the page that listed the total purchase price, and whistled.

Alan looked at Sharon and smiled.

"Now do you see how one account can be worth more than the hundred accounts I have at $2,500 dollars each? ToolTech will be worth a thousand times some of my current accounts. Does it make sense to spend more time chasing down the forty E.F. Striepeke-size accounts I have, when the sum total of them would not come close to equaling one ToolTech?"

"I see. But it just seems unbelievable. Could we really tell 95 percent of our clients to get lost?"

"I've wondered about that, too. There's no way it is going to be cost effective to go on providing the kind of service we have been providing to those smaller companies. But we could still go on selling to them. Just cut out the sales reps."

Shaking the stack of papers in his hand, Alan said, "We certainly can't go on providing this level of detail for everyone."

"No. And so many of my clients aren't big enough to ever warrant it. Most aren't even in a growth industry that could expand enough to provide a large enough base for future profitable business. Mass customization of software, or—actually—mass tailorization, if there is such a word, might be the best way to describe what we can offer our larger clients. Of course, there'll be small adjustments we can make to this overall system."

Alan nodded in agreement.

"For those smaller companies, I see us providing maybe on-line service, or telephone ordering."

"You're talking about completely revising the way this company does business," Alan said, not argumentatively, but just stating more to himself the full weight of what Sharon's proposal meant.

"Honestly, has the old way been working?"

"As I said, not for two years. Or more."

"So something has to change."

"But you're not talking about changing *something*; you're talking about changing *everything*."

"Alan, I heard a rumor once that you were an engineer. Is that true?"

"Yep. Electrical engineer. Then switched to selling the components I designed. Was made sales manager in less than a year. Got a better offer from SSI and have been here ever since. I was beginning to think my time here was about up. You are a rarity these days, Sharon. A business major who stayed in business and stuck to sales."

"Actually the undergrad degree was in art history, but what can you do with that?"

"Evidently it's given you a broader view of the world than I have."

"But as an engineer, you understand systems. Think of the sales department as just another system that needs to be re-engineered. How would you go about that?"

Alan thought for a moment and then nodded. "Have our commissioned reps spend their more valuable time on the big projects and hire hourly employees to handle the smaller orders. Good idea. It sounds like you have thought this through," but as he said it, Alan suddenly frowned.

"What's wrong?"

"I'm just wondering how some of these clients are going to take that—being shuffled off to the Internet or phone sales?"

"A lot of it's in how we sell it. We can't make them think we're downgrading them. We are upgrading them to instant access, 24-hours-a-day, to all of our products and to a help line. An e-commerce solution which empowers customers to access us and our services in a way that works best for them. No more waiting for a sales rep to call on you or call you back!"

Alan let out half a laugh. "That is what's so great about salespeople—they can make a cut in service sound like a new added benefit. We can just give it some nice name like *Insta-serve* or something."

"Exactly. Right now it's actually disruptive to some of our clients to have us call. Some of them have used our products for so long they know them better than we do. I have seen them do some amazing things with our software, tinkering with it to do all sorts of tasks. Since they know what they need and when they need it, and rather than have us waste our time and theirs with sales calls, they can order their own product directly. Then maybe we could just offer them a tech-support contract for an annual charge."

"I don't know," Alan said, scratching his head. "I wonder if our clients would feel comfortable with that sort of concept. I mean, without direct, face-to-face interaction."

"They're going to have to get used to it. It's the future. Actually it's the present. Some airlines are charging you more if you *don't* book your flight on-line."

Alan grimaced and shook his head. "I don't like it."

"Alan, two hundred years ago, people didn't trust coins. In the frontier colonies the traders used buckskins as their currency. They knew what a buck was worth in real goods, but had no idea what a Pennsylvania shilling was worth. Carrying around dead deer got a little cumbersome, so they eventually had to trust gold and silver. A hundred-and-fifty years ago, people didn't trust paper, they wanted coins. Now, more than 98 percent of the world's money does not exist at all—not even as paper. It's just an electronic impulse in transit."

"Is that true?"

"Yep. Read it on the Internet. Most money is just a coded message."

"No, I meant about where the word *buck* comes from?"

Sharon laughed. "Yes, it's amazing what you stumble across on the web on the way to look up other things. Do you know how many times Peter O'Toole was nominated for an Academy Award?"

"Uh, no. And I guess the better question is, do I care?"

"Neither did I. But anyway, like it or not, you, our customers—*everyone*—must learn to use the web effectively or get left by the side of the road on the information superhighway."

"You're right. I'll admit I've primarily just used the Internet as entertainment—certainly not business research."

"It took a 12-year-old to teach me the usefulness of the web."

Alan nodded. "I may have to rent a kid to teach me."

"I'll find out what my son charges. Plus, I get 10 percent as his agent."

"Always the salesperson, aren't you?" Alan laughed and then turned serious. "If you think about it, we've been giving away minor service and training. If we were to expand those functions, we could sell packages that could become a new source of revenue."

"Once I started looking at it that way, I realized there is a lot of potential we have been ignoring. Money left on the table."

"All this complicated software that you've worked out with engineering—how adaptable is it to other clients?"

"Somewhat."

"Somewhat?" Alan let out a full laugh. His first real laugh in what Sharon guessed were weeks, if not months. "What kind of an answer is that?"

"Somewhat of one," Sharon joked. "With minor adjustments, this set of programs could be used for almost any industrial manufacturer. Use scale as much as possible, but still customize for each company that is big enough to warrant it. That's the mass tailoring I mentioned. You see it more and more in everything from retailers of home computers to car makers."

"This software is going to be so sophisticated, I'm wondering if one rep will be able to learn the intricacies of each type of software for each type of business...."

"Or we may want to switch accounts around," Sharon said completing Alan's thought.

"So that we have a rep who specializes in a specific industry...."

"And reps will have to analyze how many of their accounts meet certain criteria—size, growth potential, et cetera. I think we need to formalize a process to see which ones meet our customer-focus profile. Sort of divide them up into companies like ToolTech that could benefit from this type of customization, and companies which could just do the on-line ordering, or whatever," Sharon said. "I've been giving this a lot of thought...."

"Go on," Alan encouraged, now willing to listen patiently to all she had to say.

"We'll probably want to look at each account carefully and sort them out," Sharon proposed. "ToolTech will be sort of a special case. It'll take so much time and so many resources that I can't see that we'll be able to develop more than one of those this year. We can make just that one company our primary focus.

"Then we'll have our 'B' list, so to speak. Clients we can close this year and who have at least $50,000 potential, and for whom 5.0 will work.

"The 'A' list will be clients with the kind of potential ToolTech has. Multi-million dollar deals which will take a long time and some research to develop as ToolTech did, and will. It could take 6 to 18 months to close those deals. Given how much time and money we'll have to devote to them, we better make very sure we're selecting the right targets. For the time being, we'll just go on servicing them the best we can, while at the same time doing background research along the way.

"I realize I made a mistake in letting some of these 'A' clients slide and will have to do some work to repair whatever damage that may have been done. As we try to expand this new system to other clients—one at a time—it's going to take some hard work to keep our remaining 'A' clients happy until we can devote our full resources to them.

"Level 'C' will be the third type of customer. Accounts like E.F. Striepeke that we'll begin handling through phone and/or Internet sales. It'll require a whole new way of looking at those clients. They are simple sales and could become a major profit center if we could cut out the sales rep's commission and time and expense. Instead of a direct rep making 2 to 5 calls per day, someone on the phone could handle 25 or even 50 contacts a day. Since our competition is eliminating their reps as well, it could get very price competitive, but if we pass along to the client some of the savings of not having reps call, and offer things like tech support and service contracts, internal sales could be quite profitable."

"We may lose some of those accounts if we stop holding their hands," Alan said. "But I guess we have to be prepared for that and assume we can make it up elsewhere."

"We may want to offer them some kind of big initial discount to get them to at least try the new way. And they'll see that if they look elsewhere for those transactions, say to Reese, that the kind of personal service they once received is gone forever. As consumers, we all complain about how bad the customer service has become in some service-oriented industries, but I guess like we're now discovering, 'automation' is the price they're willing to pay to keep the clients who really matter."

"Exactly. It may not feel good to be told you're not worthy

of their business, but it's becoming a fact of life as things move faster and faster. We may want to have some kind of client meetings or 'user golf tournaments'—or something—to maintain some human contact and tell them we still value their business and input."

"Sharon, you may not have time to take care of more accounts. ToolTech may very well keep you tied up."

"That would be fine. This deal would be worth giving up all of my other accounts."

"If you can find us deals the size of this one with ToolTech, your time and SSI's money are both better spent doing that than having you chase nickels and dimes."

They continued chattering away and missed their tee time. Alan started scribbling notes to himself, and they soon found themselves sitting in Sharon's car outlining a whole new way of doing business. As Alan was talking at one point, Sharon looked out the windshield and saw that over on the lawn, the rabbit had returned to contentedly eat his breakfast of grass. Although they never played even one hole of golf, Sharon was glad she had managed to get Alan out of the office. She had not realized just how much strain he was under until he let loose yelling at her, and how relieved he was to see that there might be a way to save the sales department and his job.

EXECUTIVE SUMMARY

Getting Aligned

Have you established allies inside your organization that will support your ideas that may threaten the existing system?

• Do you understand how your direct manager and his or her manager are measured and compensated?

• Do you invest enough time with those within your organization (allies) to communicate the issues that are surfacing with customers and competitors?

• Are your key relationships committed to your success and can you depend on their belief, trust, and support when faced with opposition in your organization?

Developing solid *"relationship strategies"* (allies) inside your own organization is vital to long-term success in a market-driven organization. Clients will require you to have the authority to marshal resources on projects that may be unique or outside the boundaries of mainstream solutions.

Before Sharon can finalize commitments with the executives of ToolTech, she must be able to gain the support of key executives within her own organization. The internal support of these key executives will give her the ability to fully deliver the solution she has promised ToolTech.

Because Sharon's clients and solutions deliver such value to her own company, she actually becomes a member of the inner circle of power and influence.

117

CHAPTER EIGHT

Grip it & rip it!

Monday morning Alan breezed into Sharon's office with a smile on his face.

"Good morning, Sharon."

His pleasant manner and greeting caught Sharon by surprise.

He smiled at her startled look. "I can honestly say this is the first time in over a year that I've looked forward to coming to work. It was so weird—I had started to hate this place, but also lived in fear of having to leave it."

Sharon, finally recovered from the shock, smiled back. "It's good to see you smiling again. I thought you'd forgotten how."

Alan laughed, "Julia, out at reception, asked me what was wrong. In the year or two she has worked here, I don't think she has ever seen me smile or had me wish her a nice day. I don't feel the least bit tired even though I stayed up half the night Saturday and last night going over the ideas and numbers you gave me. I have some thoughts and questions for you...."

Sharon removed her briefcase from her spare chair, and Alan sat down. As she did, she wondered if Alan had ever been in her office before. Alan was a man possessed.

He spent his morning with Sharon, and, at times with Vicky and Erick from engineering. If he was in Sharon's office, he seemed to need to talk to one of the engineers, and when he was downstairs with them, he was calling Sharon every five minutes.

Sharon was surprised to see how well Alan took command. She had always seen him as a rather ineffectual leader who let his subordinates, including her, walk-all-over him. But now that he had a purpose he took the lead with a boldness and decisiveness she never would have guessed he possessed.

Midmorning Sharon got an email from Alan outlining the new plan for the sales force—the same plan they had briefly detailed while sitting in her parked car at the golf course. Sharon looked at the information that appeared on her screen:

Corporate Accounts (Sharon & current sales team)
Clients with the multi-million dollar potential that will require considerable research. (As of now, just ToolTech)

Direct Sales (current sales team)
Clients who will be the market for versions 5.0 and 6.0, but have the potential to become corporate clients with custom solutions.

Telesales and Internet Sales
Clients who have developed internal expertise and can work with SSI's tech support on-line. They will continue to buy SSI upgrades such as 5.0 and 6.0, but without sales reps calling. They have little potential to ever grow to the corporate account level. (E.F. Striepeke is a good example.)

VARS (Value Added Re-Sellers)
Independent businesses that add value in the form of consulting before, during and after the implementation of 5.0 and 6.0.

Sharon studied his outline and nodded approvingly. Alan disappeared for a few hours after lunch, which made Sharon wonder what was happening, until her phone rang.

"Sharon, Alan. Could you step over to my office?"

"Of course," was all she could say before he hung up.

Alan, usually neat to the point of compulsive, sat in his office surrounded by a sea of papers. Sharon recognized many as ones she had given him and others as ones she had worked on with Erick.

"Don't touch anything," Alan said with a smile. "I have this broken down into all its components."

Sharon nodded as Alan moved a stack of papers from the chair to the floor to give her a place to sit.

"No offense to your great research and work here, Sharon, but I wanted to make sure I understood it completely and was in full possession of the facts before we take this to Ms. Washington."

Sharon's opinion of his managerial skills was elevated a little more when Alan asked her if she felt as though he were stealing her project and her idea.

"Not at all," she said. She went on to tell him how impressed she was that he had spent so much time over the weekend working on ideas to service most of their accounts via phone and Internet. "It was just a half-baked idea when I threw it out, but you've made it a solid plan. All this stuff about a 24-hour help desk, the ordering system—this is a lot of work."

Sharon assured him that he was welcome to any of her work if it would be helpful in making the plan work company-wide. She added that she certainly did not have the clout to demand a meeting with Estelle Washington or any other VP of SSI for that matter.

"Well, I can hardly demand a meeting with her, either," Alan answered. "How well do you know her?"

"Not well at all."

Alan frowned. "Ms. Washington likes things organized and set in writing. She'll hack it up and make lots of changes, but she prefers a solid document to begin with before she starts hacking. All of what I'm going to show you is really just your ideas filled out a bit. And the whole thing of re-organizing the sales force, again, is your idea in my words."

Sharon nodded.

"She's tough," Alan continued. "Sounds a lot like that VP at ToolTech you told me about. She won't see me unless I give her good cause, and then I better have facts and figures to back up whatever I'm talking about. One of the first things she did when she came here five years ago was to cut in half the number of people who report directly to her. I'm one of the chosen few, but only when I have a specific purpose."

"I guess after we each make vice-president, we can start being aloof, too," Sharon joked.

"I'm not sure you will want to be VP. If you bring in many deals like this, you will be making more than her. And I sure wouldn't want her job or her pressure. She has to be hyper-organized just to stay on top of things. She's even more systematic than I am."

Sharon winced at the thought and wondered how that could be possible.

"So I sort of understand how her mind works, at least in part," Alan went on. "I think the first step is to ask for a meeting. I want to read you the email I wrote her and see if it covers everything."

"Okay. Sure."

Alan read, "*At your earliest convenience, I would like to schedule a meeting with you to discuss major changes that I believe could greatly benefit SSI.*

"*I would like to arrange for one of our top sales reps, Sharon Kelly, to explain some ideas she has that can dramatically increase our top and bottom lines—*"

"Sorry to interrupt, but I think this would be a good time to use Ms. Washington's number."

Alan cocked his head slightly, trying to follow. "Her number?"

"The 40 percent sales increase she projected for this year," Sharon said, trying to explain. "That would get her attention right away."

"Good thinking," Alan said as he hurriedly made changes to the message.

He continued reading, backing up a bit to make sure he

had worded Sharon's changes correctly, *"I would like to arrange for one of our top sales reps, Sharon Kelly, to explain some ideas she has that will ensure we meet, if not exceed, our projected 40 percent sales increase."* Alan glanced up from the screen to see Sharon nodding approvingly. He continued, *"To explain any technical issues which may arise, I would also like to include in this meeting the Manager of Engineering, Vicky Fong, and Senior Projects Engineer, Erick McDermot, who have been working with Sharon on developing this new approach.*

"I think as the result of this meeting—"

Sharon held up a hand and Alan paused.

"Do you think it would be helpful to include Syed ... uh ... um?"

Alan furrowed his brow, confused.

"From marketing," Sharon answered to his unspoken question.

"Oh, Syed Tahilramani."

"That's him," Sharon said.

"Yes. I'll get him and Fariel from distribution to sit in as well. If we're going to spell this whole thing out to Ms. Washington, it would be a good way to get those other departments up to speed and get their buy-in as soon as possible."

Alan stroked his chin and looked out the window at the sun glinting off cars in the parking lot and then off in the distance at the cars streaming by on the 805 Freeway.

"I'm sorry to interrupt," Sharon apologized. "I hope I didn't make you lose your train of thought."

"No. I have all of that written down." He held up a page as proof. "I'm just wondering how best to handle Estelle. As I said, I sometimes know how she thinks, so I'm wondering what's best in this situation."

With a smile, Sharon commented, "It does seem a much more difficult task to sell people within this company than those outside, I ought to know."

Alan suddenly laughed. "Are you making reference to the

childish scene I created at the golf course on Saturday?"

"Oh no, not at all."

"Sharon, before we go on. Again, I'm sorry about the way I yelled at you on Saturday. That was uncalled for and unprofessional, and to do it in public like that. . ."

"You've been under a lot of pressure."

"Thank you, but still there was no excuse for that, and I'm sorry. I'm especially sorry since you came up with the idea that will save my job, and I need your help to make it work. And you have been so good about this whole thing, and not mentioning what an idiot I was and how badly I have acted."

Sharon cut him off as the apology was beginning to get embarrassing. "Someone has been extra nice to me lately, so I feel I should pass it on."

Alan smiled and thanked Sharon. Then, remembering his previous train of thought, he continued. "Well, the next piece in this puzzle is getting a meeting with Estelle."

"Is it going to be that difficult?" Sharon asked.

"Not difficult. It just has to be done in a precise way."

"So, she'll be skeptical?"

"Very skeptical. As she is of everything. That's why everything must be precise from the moment I propose the idea."

Alan leaned back in his chair, removed his glasses and rubbed his forehead. "I'm just concerned that if we bring Syed and Fariel in.... Well, you saw how angry I was when I felt you'd left me out of the loop by going to engineering without telling me."

"I realize now that was wrong..." Sharon started to apologize again.

"No, please. You tried going through me and I yelled at you. I just mention it because I don't want Estelle to feel that way, justified or not. So I think we should pitch the idea to her and let her decide when to bring in marketing and distribution."

"You know her better than I do," Sharon nodded. "And I

know I handled my pitch to you badly."

Alan shrugged it off.

"So what does the rest of the email say?" Sharon asked.

"Where was I? Let's see. Why I want to meet with her. Who will be there…. Oh yes, next, what we will talk about and what I hope will be the outcome of the meeting." Alan resumed reading, *"I would like Sharon to tell you of her recent experience with one of our major customers, ToolTech, and what that situation says about our current market conditions. I would then like to share some ideas we have as to how SSI may address those conditions, and answer any questions you may have. I think as a result of this meeting, you will be able to evaluate the ideas to create the sales growth and profitability you committed to achieve."*

Alan looked up at Sharon who nodded approval. "Sounds good."

"Anything you'd change?"

"Not a word."

"Good. I didn't read you the part about suggesting 10 a.m. tomorrow. Does that work for you?"

"Sure."

"Good." Alan swung around in his chair to face his computer and with a few keystrokes sent the message. He pivoted back to Sharon. "I think I should talk to Syed and Fariel and sort of get a feel for how well marketing and distribution could handle such a move, in case Estelle brings that up. Get some idea of where they are, how adaptable, et cetera."

Sharon nodded. "Good idea. And at least they can start thinking about what we have in mind. And since you're talking with Estelle, I'll talk with Erick."

"About?"

"Getting him to stick to the point. He's one of those people, who if you ask him what time it is, will tell you how his watch works. We just need him to answer a question and then stop talking."

"I noticed that side of him in the few chats we had this

morning," Alan agreed. "Would you like me to talk to him? As a fellow engineer, maybe I can relate to him better. I'll just encourage him to let you do most of the talking and for him to back you up by briefly answering specific questions related to his area of expertise."

"If you have time, it couldn't hurt," Sharon smiled.

"I'll make time. There's one other thing. In the part of the email to Estelle I didn't read, I also told her I would be sending along some documentation to look over before the meeting. So I'd like you to look this over. She is, as I've said, very analytical and likes all of the details; so I like to spell things out with her. Usually gets me what I want. Strangely her boss, Mr. Carlson, is just the opposite. It's made it a challenge the few times I've had to present something to both of them. And that's where this will end up, I'm sure. As I said, Estelle likes things neatly planned. So I drew up this gap analysis."

Alan handed Sharon a document.

SSI's Current Situation:

- *SSI has lost its competitive position in the marketplace due to competition and delay in the release of the new version of software.*
- *Sales reps are working harder but sales numbers are significantly off budget.*
- *SSI's new version will only bring temporary improvements in sales.*
- *Customers are in a highly volatile marketplace and need help in driving costs out of their businesses.*
- *Customer base is diverse and sales strategy doesn't differentiate type of sales interface.*
- *Sales costs are very high.*
- *SSI is losing customers to competitors; can take 2-5 years to win them back.*
- *SSI has an existing large opportunity at ToolTech in excess of $2 million.*

Desired Situation:

- *Achieve/exceed sales goals committed to by Estelle and Alan.*
- *Create a new source of sustainable differentiation.*
- *Grow top line and bottom line in sales.*
- *Grow customer satisfaction level and customer retention.*
- *Reduce costs of sales.*
- *Develop a market-driven approach for product development.*
- *Leverage ToolTech opportunity to restructure sales, product development, and operations for growth.*

*   *   *   *   *   *   *   *   *   *   *   *

It was after 1 p.m. when the 10 a.m. meeting with Estelle Washington finally ended. Washington asked more challenging questions than expected and was more thorough than the VP at ToolTech. Sharon was again surprised at how difficult it was to sell within her own company as compared to that of selling in the capacity of an outside expert for a client. At ToolTech, Sharon had the confidence of knowing the product better than the people to whom she was selling. Now she was talking about changing a company to the people near the highest echelon of that company who may have a vested interest in seeing that things stayed the same.

She was also surprised at what a good team she and Alan made. With perfect precision, Alan would turn half the questions over to Sharon to answer, only jumping back in to field questions relating to topics Sharon felt were out of her area of familiarity, such as re-organizing parts of the sales force.

Ms. Washington never once smiled or gave any other sign of approval throughout the entire meeting. Sharon had made many a sales call in her day and thought she was good at gauging when she had the client sold—when their body language and tone of voice said *yes*—even if the client was still asking questions. This one was different. Estelle Washington was looking at her watch the whole time they were in her office.

As Ms. Washington ushered them out of her office, Alan felt the need to try to get some kind of a feeling as to how the meeting had gone, since his boss had still shown not the slightest hint of enthusiasm. "A lot of work went into this," he said to Estelle.

"I can see that," she said coolly.

"Mainly Sharon's work," Alan added.

"Actually, as far as the software goes, mainly Erick's work. Just my idea," Sharon amended.

"Whoever," she said, still unsmiling.

"Honestly, it was a pleasure to get out of my rut," Erick said. "I think we all tend to take our jobs for granted. We do the same old thing and we're tempted to just sleepwalk through it. It's nice to feel like what I am doing matters again."

"Amen to that. . .," Alan seconded.

"It's going to take me a while to look all this over," Estelle interrupted. "I'll get back to you."

On the elevator, Erick said, "That seemed to go well." Sharon looked at him for any indication that he meant it sarcastically. Surprisingly to Sharon, Erick didn't seem to have noticed Estelle's cool reception.

When the doors opened on their floor, both Alan and Sharon said quiet good-byes to the engineers who stayed on to ride back to their basement.

After the doors closed, Alan said, "That Erick gets a little wound up doesn't he?"

"Yes, he does like to talk. I had the same problem with him at ToolTech. I shouldn't say problem, since his enthusiasm is great and I need his technical expertise."

"We just still need to find his *off* button," Alan laughed. "Maybe I should have another talk with him."

"I couldn't agree more." Sharon shared the laugh.

"With this new way of doing things, I guess we're going to

have to train everyone in how to move to the "ask" and "listen" mode. If you think about it, anyone who interacts with clients—in any way—is in sales."

"True. Fortunately, Erick's enthusiasm hasn't really hurt the process so far. But, in some instances, one wrong word from an engineer could kill a sale."

"I wish some of his zeal had rubbed off on Estelle," Alan sighed.

"Did you notice the difference in the questions she asked Erick and Vicky, and the questions she asked you and me? Especially me."

Alan reflected for a moment.

Sharon went on, "She assumed Vicky and Erick had the technical expertise to know if this was at all feasible. She trusted them to give her the straight info and just accepted it as the correct answer. She would ask me a question, then look through the documentation to confirm it. She didn't do that with Erick."

"That's true, but I didn't notice it in the meeting. I think it's typical of her analytical style."

"She was just double checking. I'm used to it, so I don't resent it when people want to see things in writing. It's part of being in sales. If you sound the least bit reluctant to let them check, they become uncomfortable because accuracy and data are high priorities in their decision-making process."

"So what do we do about it?" questioned Alan.

"Let her look it all over and draw her own conclusions. She hasn't said *no* or anything close to *no*. So it's a little premature to panic. As you said, she likes to analyze. So let her. I think she's a smart enough woman to see the logic of the plan after she reads it all."

"Change is scary," Alan sighed.

"We'll have to give her a *little* time—I emphasize little. Truth is, we don't have that much time. I'll need the weight of senior management behind me to get to the top at ToolTech. So how about we give her a couple of days, and if we don't have a green light yet, I'll get someone over at ToolTech to call her."

"Isn't that a little weird? Asking a customer to do inside sales for you?"

"It won't really be sales. Just a confirmation call of sorts. I know Lorenzo Ortiz would be happy to do it. He really wants this new software. And wants it yesterday! The people at ToolTech definitely see the value. And, if they do, how can she say *no*? And if necessary I'll get their VP to talk to her. VP to VP. They have to speak to each other, right? That'll have to carry some clout. But I don't see it coming to that."

"Grip it and rip it"

Can you sell your solution
inside your own organization?

- Do you know how your manager is being measured? Is it around performance?
- How does your solution impact your organization, and can you quantify its potential value?
- Who in your organization stands to gain the most if your solution is implemented?
- Who in your organization stands to lose the most if your solution is implemented?
- Can you help these people by repositioning the change into an opportunity?

Just as it was important that Sharon be able to craft a compelling business solution for ToolTech, she now, with the sponsorship of her manager, Jeff, needs to be able to create an equally compelling business solution for her own organization.

Salespeople, fully knowledgeable of their surroundings, must continually be able to sell solutions both internally and externally. This includes having the ability to define the win-win-win component of a solution while carefully detailing the ways in which everyone involved will realize success.

Fortunately, Sharon's confidence in the economic contribution of her solution to ToolTech's business goals, gives her the momentum needed to overcome the fear of pushing forward when faced with major obstacles.

CHAPTER NINE

The approach shot

The following day, Tuesday, Alan and Sharon stewed in silence with no word from Estelle Washington.

Sharon spent Wednesday morning and early afternoon working with Jeff Lee and Bill Atkinson, ironing out more details about ToolTech's software. She found herself discussing a service package. She wasn't sure how they would do this, but when Atkinson asked for help, she knew she would have to find a way to provide it. She also wondered, even as she was talking about expanding the ToolTech deal, if Ms. Washington was disassembling it. She felt better working than just waiting for word, and there was still much to be done at ToolTech.

When Sharon's pager vibrated during the meeting, she jumped—just as she had the first day she ever wore it—when its buzzing on her belt startled her. She looked down and saw it was Alan's phone number and coded 'urgent.' As quickly as she could find a convenient stopping point in the meeting, she wrapped things up, excused herself and asked Jeff if she could use the phone in his office.

"What took you so long?" Alan asked as soon as he heard her voice. But before Sharon could answer, he said, "Never mind. I got an email from Estelle."

"And?"

"It's a go! She is so—," Alan began, then, deciding to hold his tongue, continued. "Well, never mind that, either. The email just says, '*Proceed with ToolTech plans. Engineering has been instructed to cooperate fully. Other aspects of planned reorganization are under review.*'"

"Great. Not exactly the backslap we had hoped for, but we're on our way." Sharon let out a sigh of relief.

"Yep. And I'm sure she's just rewriting our plan to make it her own, but at least we got stage one approved," Alan said, the relief evident in his voice.

"I've never gotten an email from her that was not some department-wide directive. How do you interpret that? You have freedom to do whatever?"

"What *whatever*?"

"ToolTech is asking about a service contract."

"Have you talked numbers with them?"

"Not yet," Sharon said.

"Don't. Leave it vague. Let me make some calls and do some checking. Estelle wants to set up a meeting with you, the engineers, marketing, and distribution and get everyone on board and up to speed before we take this to Mr. Carlson."

"I see."

"He really likes to have everybody happy. I swear sometimes in meetings he's going to suggest a group hug, or that we all join hands and sing some campfire song." Alan did a Mr. Rogers-like voice, "Fariel, do you want to add anything? Estelle, are you okay with this? Syed, any other questions...."

Sharon laughed. She hadn't known Alan had a sense of humor.

Alan was laughing also, and said, "Of course, Estelle is tearing her hair out while he's doing this, but she somehow manages to conform to his style enough to get what she wants with him. She'd like this meeting today if possible. Actually, knowing her she'd like it *yesterday*, but since I doubt that's possible, can you be back this afternoon?"

"I could be back by say, three?"

"Sounds good."

*   *   *   *   *   *   *   *   *   *   *   *

For the next two weeks, Sharon found herself spending more and more time at ToolTech in meetings with Jeff, Lorenzo

Ortiz, Bill Atkinson and other key individuals at their company. She made no other client sales calls at all, because the rest of her time was spent working with Erick, Vicky, and Alan.

Engineering now had all the frantic activity of a retail store the day after Christmas. They were interviewing and hiring new people, and throwing themselves with new vigor into finishing 5.0 now that they could see how vital it was to all of SSI's new plans. It was not just an exercise in futility, but the cornerstone of the new operation. They knew that regular software updates are the mainstay of any software seller. Sharon's special project with ToolTech was seen now as a source of new leading-edge modular updates of their brand products that they had been selling. Perhaps they would call it Enterprise 2.0, since it was so far above their current version. It was far too sophisticated for many of their other clients' needs.

Alan had latched on to the service idea, and was running with it. He drew up plans for Sharon to take to ToolTech. Sharon and Alan worked together on the fly, shooting brief emails and phone messages to each other. The many aspects of the plan all began to solidify in a way she would not have thought possible, given how little time they had to develop it.

Sharon had to call and cancel her weekly golf dates with Joan both weeks. Joan was her usual understanding self, and congratulated Sharon on all that was in the works. She added, "It sounds like you're planning for D-Day."

"It sure feels like it."

* * * * * * * * * * * *

On Saturday, Sharon took a break from work and attended Max's soccer game.

Jeff and his wife, Jackie, came to watch their son, Ben, play.

After the game, Jeff took Sharon aside. "I sort of have a problem."

"Oh?"

"Its name is Ann."

"Uh oh."

"She went to her boss and told him that I was running around doing everything but my job."

"If I remember your organizational chart, isn't that Mr. Atkinson?"

"Yep."

"So, can't you talk to him?"

"I can. But do I want to? She is already feeling like she is being left out of the loop...."

"Not to sound heartless, but her choice, as I recall."

"Yes, but if I go that far above her head, I may not just be burning a bridge, I may be torching an entire village. I think there will be serious fallout."

"Could she fire you?"

"I don't think she has that power anymore. But she could get fired. And that could create a lot of bad feelings all over the place. And I kind of think it makes me look bad in the process. I'd really like to solve this just between Ann and me, if I can."

"Hmmm."

"I'd like your help with some sort of a plan to handle Ann. You seem to work with Alan so well now."

"*Now* is the keyword," Sharon laughed. "You didn't see the fireworks we went through to get to this point."

"I doubt Ann or I can survive any fireworks. One or the other of us would not be standing when the smoke clears, I'm afraid. I could just ignore her and trust that it'll be her, not me, that goes. But we were friends. Or, at least, friendly. I'd like to salvage some of that if I can."

Sharon nodded.

Jeff went on, "You saved my job; I'd like to save hers. She's not a bad person. Just an ineffective leader. I'm not sure she appreciates how precarious her position is. After TT and CTC finish this merger, if she looks like she's not a team player, hers could be one of the jobs eliminated."

"That wouldn't be good."

"So, can we talk?"

"Of course. When and where?"

"We really can't talk at my office, for obvious reasons."

"And my office is a complete zoo these days."

"How 'bout playing nine, Thursday afternoon?"

Before Sharon could answer, Jeff continued with his own sales-pitch trying to justify the game, "It'll give us a chance to talk, and you said yourself you haven't played in weeks. You don't want to look bad at the tournament this Saturday, do you? I sure don't."

"You're right. Mind if I call Joan and ask her to join us? I've ducked my game with her for weeks. She's been so nice to me, and I feel guilty. Like I'm avoiding her."

"No, not at all. I enjoyed the last round we played with her. She came up with a few gems of wisdom."

"And has had plenty more for me, since."

On the drive home from the soccer game, Sharon asked Max, "Up for ice cream?"

"Sure."

"Too bad that goalie stopped your shot. That was a nice pass and a nice kick."

"He's good. I couldn't believe he made it all the way back across to grab it. I think he's the best goalie in the league."

"You'll get 'em next time. Listen, I'm sorry I've been so busy lately. Things'll get better soon, I promise. I may be a little late getting home Monday. Ben's dad and I need to plan a little strategy, so we're going to play a little golf after work. Do you mind?"

"Nah. I understand. This is a big deal you're working on."

"The biggest. And you've been a huge help. So you can get a ride with Artie's mom?"

"No prob."

"Call and make sure, okay?"

"Sure."

"Things are going to be a little tight time- and money-wise until this deal closes...."

"I understand...."

"Thank you. It's really nice to know I can count on you." She clasped his shoulder. "So, two promises. One. A weekend away. As soon as school is out, you pick where you want to go. Disneyland? DisneyWorld? And I know you wanted to do Huntsville."

"Cool!"

"And," she began, "start reading up on DVD players, so we'll know which one to buy."

"Are you serious?"

"I couldn't have done it without you. So research a good one, and we'll get it. We'll also have to do whatever it is you wanted to do to update or expand the computer."

"Awesome!"

*   *   *   *   *   *   *   *   *   *   *   *

The following day, Monday morning, Alan walked into Sharon's office without knocking. He dropped a bound report on her desk.

"Check it out," he said disgustedly.

"What is it?" Sharon asked, picking it up and reading the title page aloud. "Software Solutions, Inc., Sales Force 21st Century."

"As I predicted. She rewrote our plan and gave us zero credit. But wants to do it all just as we proposed."

"I guess the important thing is that we got what we wanted. And what the company needs."

"You started the whole thing, the least she could do—"

Sharon could see he was building to a boil as he had in the golf course parking lot, so she interrupted, "Alan, look at it this way. There are a few ways a company can reward its employees: money, promotions, credit. We have the power to make the changes we need. We will both make a lot of money when this goes through, so if we don't get the credit, what's the big deal? And usually what goes around comes around. Let's wait and see what happens."

"You sure are taking this well."

"Again, what's the alternative?"

"I have a good mind to tell her—"

"Tell her what? You could get yourself fired. After you've waited and sweated for things to turn around, and now that they will—lose your job? That wouldn't be good. Or she might just end up distrusting the sales department, and that could make things difficult, at best."

"Or you could wait to see what happens, as Sharon suggested."

Alan and Sharon were both stunned to see Estelle standing in the doorway.

Both Sharon's and Alan's jaws were too slack for them to speak. Estelle had never been to Sharon's corner of the floor, or even on the floor, except to go to Alan's office at the opposite end, so it never occurred to them to close the door.

"Your names don't appear on it because Mr. Carlson, who will have to approve such a major restructuring, is going to have to see that everyone in all departments approves. He likes me and trusts my judgment. I want this plan approved ASAP," She pronounced it like a word, *A-sap*. "So I want it to look like a team project all the way. After it is approved and working, then I intend to tell him where it came from, and if it works, figure out a bonus package."

Alan looked at Sharon, embarrassed.

"You'll note in there I mention a 'Customer Relationship Manager' position. That will be you, Alan, with a commensurate raise in pay. Sharon, the position of Business Development Leader is yours. Since you started this whole thing, and we're going to need your input all along the way, you might as well be compensated for it. I'm hoping you two will look that over immediately and make any comments or corrections. I've also given copies to marketing, distribution, and all concerned parties for their input. I want to make sure everyone gives it the green light before Mr. Carlson starts asking questions. I'd like to have it on the president's desk no later than Monday."

Alan and Sharon were still too dumbfounded to speak, so Estelle went on, "The traditional approach to sales development simply isn't working. I want to get started retraining and restructuring sales immediately. I can imagine we will be seeing very little of some of the reps from now on and it will just be more efficient for them to work from home. It's going to take a much longer time to make these new sales. Other reps will continue to work on the 'B' accounts still selling them 4.0, and then 5.0 as soon as it is ready, while they learn to be more consultative. They will have to slowly start reducing the number of accounts they have to be able to bring greater focus on the ones they keep."

Again both Alan and Sharon were stunned into silence.

Facing the open door, Sharon could see that the people walking by were as stunned to see Estelle in her office as she was. Many slowed to watch and try to catch some of what was going on. Sharon casually got up and closed the door, not wanting anyone else to overhear anything they should not.

"I know Mr. Carlson will approve the plan. We will hold off on the bigger projects, such as starting the inside sales department, until we have the official green light from him, but I want to begin to makes changes within your department immediately, Alan. There are already rumors starting and I would rather tell everyone what is happening, as Vicky did in engineering, rather than have people hear from someone who heard it from someone who heard from engineering. So we need a meeting with your reps, next week if possible, to be able to communicate with them and get their buy-in as soon as possible. And I will want input from both of you for the web page

I have ordered engineering to begin developing. How soon can you be ready to brief your reps?"

Alan's shock finally wore off enough to say something. "I can see we may have a problem there."

"How so?"

"I was reluctant to believe Sharon when she said she could give up clients and make more sales. That makes zero sense on the surface. And I can see some of our reps questioning that and not wanting their accounts taken from them and given to an inside sales department. We're going to have to prepare well for this announcement so as not to scare anyone."

Sharon nodded.

Estelle said, "But that doesn't make sense. When I saw what—no offense—what Sharon's commission will be on this, it floored me. Not that it's not worth it, but this one check will be more than we've ever paid a rep in an entire *year*."

"If you had told me I was being replaced by an order-entry department, I would have been a little upset," Sharon said, adding weight to Alan's concerns.

"I plan to hold Sharon up as exhibit 'A' of what's possible under this new system," Alan said. "Still it could take months or a year to make one sale this size. It'll be worth it when it happens, but I'm not sure some of them will want to quit schmoozing and golfing long enough to do the in-depth research, and concentrated effort necessary to put a deal like this together."

Sharon looked at Alan and mouthed 'Keith.'

Alan nodded. "We have one rep. He is older, just a few years from retirement. I'm not sure how much he is going to want to make such a big adjustment."

"I see. We need to give everyone the opportunity to make the change."

"Oh, absolutely. I'm just thinking out loud, that maybe we might want to have some kind of early retirement package ready for him, in case. Everyone else is about Sharon's age. If they can't make the transition, we will have to see if there is some new job for them here, or let them go."

Alan continued, "The other thing we have to work on is the service agreement Sharon proposed."

"I hope I didn't throw you a curve with that," Sharon said apologetically.

"You did," Estelle answered. "But that's okay. It's a good time to think of those things before we get too far along. It's not going to be enough to just sell these people a software program and walk away. Sometimes the most critical phase of a sale is maintaining the customer's faith in you *after* the sale."

"True," Alan agreed. "Often salespeople are so excited they got in the door, and that the customer listened and then signed, they forget to support the sale afterwards. They don't remember to manage the implementation."

"I needed Erick to be completely in step with our program," Sharon said. "But, I also need all of the training or support or service people to know what we are doing as well. As Alan and I discussed, anyone who talks to a customer is in sales."

"This first deal with ToolTech is going to be particularly important, because lots of people besides ToolTech will be anxious to see how it comes out. All of our other clients will be looking at it as a reference point," Estelle agreed.

"And," Alan began, "even our other reps, and engineering people, are going to be watching to see what happens. We're asking for some major shifts and a lot of work from these people. If this new program doesn't come off without a hitch, they're going to be very reluctant to let go of their old way of doing things."

Sharon laughed. "I think engineering lost faith in 5.0 for a while, but now that they can see it's part of a larger whole, they've been re-energized."

"Sharon, I would like you and Alan to work with Vicky on what is really needed to make 5.0 work in such a way that it's going to keep our current customers happy. Software upgrades are still going to be the bread-and-butter of SSI, so to speak. Erick will be handling this new 'corporate' software with ToolTech, so Vicky will be assigning another engineer to be primarily responsible for getting 5.0 back on track. Now that we have a dialogue going on between sales and engineering, I'd like to encourage it and find out what is wrong with 5.0 and see what it needs to get it into the marketplace."

"Okay," Sharon agreed. Then, bringing up Alan's previous concern, Sharon continued. "And as far as the sales reps are concerned, Alan's right. If they don't see a way to learn and grow and increase income from having fewer clients, they're not going to want to make these major changes. This could be a rocky transition if we don't handle it just right."

"We're going to need to reassure everyone that these changes are for the best, and build some sort of team spirit. That has been sorely lacking between most departments, and even within the sales department," Estelle suggested.

"I think we need to handle the sales team with kid gloves," Alan said. "No offense, Sharon, but ego is part of what makes so many of these people so good. People resist change anyway so we need a plan to get these people to buy-in."

"I'm thinking focus groups," Estelle said. "Present the market data that you two have prepared, let the salespeople see how credible it is, and they can add their own numbers from their own experience, so they understand why these changes are necessary. We need their help to paint a new vision of how sales will change and grow. We need to re-inspire them to sell 4.0 and the upgrades when they are available as they learn to handle expanded 'corporate' clients. The transition will require some new skills. Getting them to add business value to simple solutions while learning how to sell the complex solutions to higher rungs of the customer's company. We need to use the same gap analysis you used with me. They will more than likely arrive at the same conclusions we have. If they do, then they will really own the solution. If not, we'll get some additional ideas. Just as Sharon had to sell the plan to you, Alan, and you both had to sell it to me, we all need to sell it to Mr. Carlson and to the other reps."

Alan nodded. "We're dealing with a bright group of people. Once they do their own analysis, I think they'll come to the same conclusion Sharon did. Once they identify their key clients with major income potential, they'll gladly turn over their other accounts to Internet and phone sales and VARS."

"I want to stay on top of this. People have a tendency to catastrophise a future scenario. We need to tell them the truth before the rumor mill is grinding away much longer."

"True," Sharon agreed. "Fear makes you imagine scary things that stalk you at night."

"During these focus groups, I think it would be helpful to let them share what's been going on with them and let them vent some of their past frustrations," Alan suggested.

Estelle grimaced. "I agree it's important, but I don't want to spend too much time on this."

Alan shook his head. "I don't know that we have much choice but to spend whatever time it takes. Too often companies don't do this and people exhibit exit behavior. They either quit and leave or they quit and stay."

"Quit and stay?" Sharon asked.

"Yes, they stick around and spend their time hiding. You know the old saying, *'If you're not part of the solution, you are part of the problem.'* Worse than doing nothing, some people are so resistant to change, they will sabotage it—deliberately or subconsciously—it doesn't matter which—to try to maintain the status quo rather than adapt."

Estelle seemed unconvinced, so Alan went on, becoming, Sharon observed, the salesperson he once was. "If you have a ten-person outrigger canoe, which is going to take us in the direction we want to go the fastest? Let everyone see the benefit of where we are going so they're willing to paddle, or just order them to paddle? If they know nothing about where they are going or why, they're not likely to work hard, if at all, toward a goal they can't envision. The quit-and-stayers. Or worse, they could back-paddle and work against the rest of us because they are so afraid of the new lands and the journey across the uncharted waters that the bad place seems worth clinging to."

Sharon nodded. "If we can get them to see the same sort of solutions we did, they'll go eagerly, and row hard. A little time spent now, will save a lot of effort later. Just using this process will help demonstrate to them how this consultative approach and discovery process can work with their clients as well."

There was a silence, but already Sharon and Alan knew it was not an empty silence. It was Estelle evaluating and calculating and digesting the input she had just received.

"You're right. If we're going to take the time to do this, we should take the time to do it right. Give them a chance to vent."

Alan's sigh of relief was louder than he would have wished.

Sharon smiled.

"We need a plan to grow and expand just as soon as each phase of the plan is complete," Estelle said as she turned to leave. "So both of you read what I've put together. Please. And make notes. Lots of notes. Then we'll set up a meeting with all concerned parties and finalize a version to take upstairs."

She handed Sharon a copy of the report, opened the door and left. Alan smiled at Sharon, took his copy, saluted Sharon with it, and followed Estelle.

Sharon quickly glanced at her watch, making a mental note of her afternoon golf date with Jeff. Then, leaning back in her chair, she opened her report, picked up a pen, and began reading.

The approach shot

**Can you put together and lead an
effective team that can "win" the opportunity?**

- Does this opportunity merit the resource allocation required to put a solution together?
- Have you mapped your own organizational (your team) chart and identified who will be involved, and what their roles will be?
- Do you know the styles and expertise of all your team players?
- Has your team developed a mission statement and goals for this opportunity?
- Do you have the appropriate senior executives on your team?
- Have you assessed the short-term and long-term profit potential for this account?

In the role of a consultant, a salesperson's task does not end with the creation of compelling business solutions. In fact, the role of a sales "consultant" is just beginning.

With solutions in hand, effective sales consultants will follow a plan from beginning to end. While all sales consultants should be effective in the task of delegating specialized components of a solution, they should continually work close with senior executives in overseeing the full implementation of their solutions.

Sharon is well aware of the importance of executive support for the successful implementation of her solution. Even with executive approval, however, her task is not complete. Now, she and the senior executives of SSI are given the task of assembling a team comprising the expertise and interpersonal skills needed to successfully interface with the customer's team.

CHAPTER TEN

On the green

Later that afternoon, on the golf course, Joan greeted Sharon and Jeff with her usual smile.

"So nice to see you again, Jeff."

"You may not think so after we bore you with shop talk," Sharon joked. "But don't say I didn't warn you on the phone."

"That's fine. I knew what I was getting into. And it wouldn't seem like a golf game with Sharon if we didn't talk business."

"More like you listening to me go on about my crisis du jour."

"But today the crisis is mine," Jeff volunteered.

"It's so nice of Sharon to share like that," the older woman kidded.

After their drives off the first tee, Sharon asked, "So, your boss hasn't wanted to hear about this new project, but resents that you're in on it?"

"That's about the size of it. I tried to approach her initially but she put me off, saying she needed some time to think about it. She wouldn't listen to me when I explained that we didn't have time."

"Changes happen so fast these days that you don't always have time to mull things over," Joan suggested. "You've got to have the ability—and sensibility, I might add—to act decisively, or get left behind." Joan commented.

Jeff said, "The speed of change at my company is soon going to rival that of a tornado, but I don't think my boss is willing to open her eyes to even see the funnel clouds."

"Some people thrive on change. Others run from it," Sharon answered as they all prepared to play their second shots from mid-fairway.

"And some didn't really have a choice. I think my mother

145

lived in the most interesting era," Joan commented. "They went from a time when hardly anyone had electricity or indoor plumbing to a time when every house had those, plus television. She watched the advent of cars, airplanes.... She saw telephones and radio become part of our everyday lives. She lived to see man walk on the moon."

Joan continued, almost marveling in the speed at which times had changed, "I remember, even when I was a kid, planes were so rare that when you heard one, you'd run outside to look up and watch it fly over."

Sharon and Jeff, both several decades younger than Joan, smiled at the thought.

"Changes used to take a long time to seep in, so we could get used to the idea," Joan said as she pulled her putter out of her bag. "It took 200 years for indoor plumbing to catch on— 100 years for electricity. Self-propelled vehicles were around for 50 years until they were made practical enough and desirable enough that everyone had to have a car.

"Now, my son-in-law tells me I need a new faster processor on my computer. The other one is only six months old, but he says it's obsolete. I told him I can't keep up with the one I have," Joan said, sharing a laugh with Sharon and Jeff.

Throughout the golf game, Joan continued to share her thoughts with Jeff and Sharon, and Sharon made a few suggestions as to how Jeff might try to talk with Ann.

*   *   *   *   *   *   *   *   *   *   *   *

Jeff got his chance sooner than he thought. He could tell from the way Ann pounced on him when he got off the elevator that she had been waiting for him to arrive. He tried to casually look at his watch to make sure he was not late. At the same time he wondered if things had deteriorated so badly between them that she could possibly *want* to reprimand him for being late. Even if he were late, it wasn't by more than a few minutes. His son Ben's forgotten homework project had forced him to double back home, throwing off his tightly-timed morning routine.

"May I see you in my office at your earliest convenience?" Ann said in a tone that meant NOW.

Jeff did not even bother to drop his briefcase and jacket in his office, but instead followed Ann into hers.

"What is this?" she asked handing him a piece of paper.

Jeff set down his briefcase and looked it over. It was a memo to Ann from Bill Atkinson saying that Jeff was being taken out of Ann's area, and was to head up a new staff that would coordinate all of the aspects of the new software integration and training. Atkinson and Ortiz had discussed such a move with Jeff, but this was the first he knew it was official.

Jeff read it over and looked up at Ann. As happy as this made Jeff—a promotion and raise were part of this move—he could hardly celebrate while Ann was glowering at him.

"Nice of you to tell me, Jeff."

"I didn't know when this was going to happen—*or even if it would happen*. Sorry you heard about it this way."

Ann started several sentences before picking one. "I just want you to know how badly I think you have handled this. You know there is such a thing as chain of command...."

"I asked for your help in taking this plan upstairs...."

"And when I wanted to wait and have time to look things over, you pulled this sneaky little thing behind my back, going off to other departments—"

"Ann, I did not sneak. I wanted your help, but you wouldn't give it."

"Decisions like this should be made first in purchasing!"

"Ann, the world, and this company, are changing faster than job titles and this company's bureaucracy can. Even a company as big as ours cannot look to having strength in just being big any more. Not when little people can compete so easily now."

Ann continued glaring at him, so he went on, "There just isn't time for top-down, bottom-up communication anymore. People have to be ready to go where they're needed and do what is needed. You read the memo. I don't even have a job title yet and this team I'm heading up doesn't have a name yet. It consists of whoever needs to be on it in whatever capacity for as long as they're needed.

"As this merger moves along, there're going to be a lot more changes, not less. And those changes are going to happen pretty fast. If you want to continue spending as much time making a decision as you have in the past, the decision will be made by someone else and you'll be left out."

"Is that a threat? You may have gotten a big promotion, but I don't know that you are yet in a position to threaten my job!"

"It was not a threat. It was a statement of reality. If you focus so much energy on holding on to avoid slipping down, that almost means you're stuck and aren't free to move up. You used to surf, right?"

"What?"

"When we shared an office, we used to talk about us both growing up in the South Bay up in L.A. and going surfing. That we probably were on some of the same beaches at the same time."

Ann was too surprised by the sudden change of topic to answer.

"There's one optimum time to catch a wave, right?" Jeff asked, trying to get some sort of buy-in from Ann.

He got none. So he went on, "If you're too early, the wave breaks over you and you get munched—you and your board drilled into the bottom." Ann still said nothing. So, again he pressed on, "You know, the washing machine—"

"I'm really not in the mood for a trip down memory lane," Ann snapped. "I'm a lot more concerned about my future than my past right now!"

"Please, Ann, let me finish," he said politely but firmly. "If you're too late, the wave passes you by and you slip off the backside as the surfers who caught the wave ride into shore standing on their boards."

Ann watched him as a snake would watch its prey while waiting for the moment to strike.

"Can you argue with the ocean, or get it to change the timing of the waves?"

Ann furrowed her brow and did not even bother to answer what was obviously a rhetorical question.

"Ann, there's a time to catch the wave, and that time is now. The things that're already happening and are going to happen are too big for me to change or slow down. All I can do is try to ride them out as best I can, and, if things go well, ride the crest to the beach. I'm not threatening you. I wouldn't even if I had the power to. The ocean doesn't threaten surfers. It simply is. Those who know how to surf see a big swell as an opportunity, and a chance to challenge it, conquer it, and come out ahead. Those who can't surf, fear the big waves and drown. I'm not the ocean; I'm just another surfer. Things are well beyond my control.

"I just hope you can see the opportunity here instead of being afraid of the wave. Having someone in purchasing who understands how things will work is going to be vital to getting my job done. We used to work well together. I'm hoping we can again. If not, I can't say what'll happen, but please don't blame me if you miss the wave."

*   *   *   *   *   *   *   *   *   *   *   *

Jeff called Sharon to tell her that most of their planning of how to handle Ann was for naught. "I guess all this change is happening more quickly than even we thought," he said after he told Sharon about the disastrous meeting with Ann.

"Sorry you had to hear about your new position in that sort

of environment," Sharon said apologetically. Then, with a smile in her voice, she added, "Congratulations wouldn't be out of place in this instance, I hope."

"No, not at all. And, thank you," Jeff responded, with a little more cheer in his voice. "The funny thing is, I don't even know what my new title will be. I just sort of created my own position out of thin air. Or, I should say, you did. I don't know who my team will be, or what department they'll come from, or what department I'm in now for that matter."

"Sounds like you don't know much," Sharon joked.

"Something else I don't know is how I went from minding my own business one day, hiding out in purchasing, turning down one deal with you to—a few weeks later—answering directly to no one other than Mr. Atkinson, who has not spoken to anyone since 1962, and racing around like a one-man Indy pit crew! It felt good when I called Monica at LatCo to tell her the deal was off."

"That'll teach you not to say *no* to a deal with me," she suggested.

"It's pretty amazing. There just hasn't been time to define things like a job title; we've been moving too fast—nor, does it seem to matter. As you found out, finding people in the organization who can get the job done is more important than their title or their position on a company chart."

"I think that's the way business in general is going," Sharon said. "There just isn't time anymore for strictly defined roles and departments."

"I owe you a lot, Sharon. This is a golden opportunity you've dumped in my lap, but Atkinson's memo just made me realize how much work this is going to be."

"It's not as though all of these changes are going to happen overnight. Don't look too much at the big picture or it will overwhelm you the way it almost did me. It'll take time to get the new system in place. In the meantime, we'll have to run both systems side-by-side. Keep using each old method until each department can be trained and converted. As we discussed last week, parts of this will take months. Full implementation may very well take more than a year. And that's *if* your president, board, and everyone else who still has to say *yes*, does."

"Yes, I know. But with this much momentum behind it, how can they say no? And it'll be worth it for ToolTech and for me personally. After I got passed over for Ann's job, I was sort of beginning to worry that I was going to be stuck in purchasing forever. I think you put me back on the fast track again."

"Let's hope so. I'll see you in a little bit. I'll be over with the 'gang' in about an hour."

Privately, between the two of them, Jeff had jokingly taken to calling Sharon's sales team her "gang" or "posse." Once he had remarked she had become SSI's superstar, complete with entourage. At least half of the time when she went to ToolTech now, which was quite often, she took someone along with her. Today was typical: Erick and Vicky from engineering, and Alan. Sometimes the team would fan out: Sharon meeting with Jeff; Alan with Lorenzo Ortiz; and Erick and/or Vicky with ToolTech's information systems people. A few times Estelle Washington had come along and met with Bill Atkinson.

Sharon found it a little nerve-racking at first to have to brief the always-meticulous Ms. Washington before these meetings. Even Estelle acknowledged that Sharon was the coach of this team and responsible for seeing that everyone stuck to the same message. They could not afford to send mixed signals in a deal this big. Other times there were large group discussions between the key players from ToolTech and SSI. Estelle had insisted that Sharon and Alan put the corporate goals and a mission statement in writing. She wanted to avoid sending mixed messages at all costs.

Although things seemed to be moving forward, the sale to ToolTech, which at this point was pretty much represented in the person of Bill Atkinson, was an ongoing process. She had waited for approval from above before for some large orders before, but never had had to go on selling and selling. Actually it was not even selling in the traditional sense, but more of an unending stream of questions and concerns. Those other times the people had said *yes* and were really just waiting for the money and blessing from above. This time, it was far from a done deal, and the slightest misstep of anyone from SSI talking to anyone from ToolTech could upset the whole operation.

She remembered years ago, at her first job at Scarleton, they sometimes used sales teams, but those teams were set in stone. Her team was now completely fluid, borrowing whatever personnel necessary to get the job done and address the issue of the day. Even Michael Carlson, the president of Software Solutions, Inc., made it clear he was at her disposal if need be.

At times, the unfolding of this deal with ToolTech reminded her of how she felt watching Max grow up. Like her son, the project had begun to take on a shape and a personality and a life all its own which she was no longer able to or capable of completely controlling. At other times she felt like a football coach sending in whatever special team player who was needed at the moment. Most of the time she thought of Jeff Lee and Lorenzo Ortiz more as members of her team than of ToolTech's. They wanted this deal as much as she did. Maybe more. As insiders they could go places and talk to people with a freedom that she could never have. Bill Atkinson remained difficult to approach, but Ortiz always managed to find a way when Sharon needed to see the elusive VP.

She was spending enough time at ToolTech that Jeff had found her an empty office on his floor to use. In spite of the pressure she could feel from both companies' vice-presidents, her sales intuition told her that things were falling in place for a final agreement soon.

*　　*　　*　　*　　*　　*　　*　　*　　*　　*　　*　　*

Sharon and Alan had a lot of work to do to prepare for the meeting Estelle had scheduled for a week from Thursday with all of the reps.

Once again, Sharon had to call Joan and cancel their weekly golf date. Sharon apologized profusely, but Joan, as usual, took it in stride.

"Have you heard any word from Jeff—since our golf game Monday?" Joan asked before hanging up.

"As a matter of fact, yes." Sharon went on to tell Joan about Jeff's confrontation with his boss.

"Sorry to hear about that. Conflict is always difficult." Then, adding, "But I'm thrilled to hear about Jeff's promotion. You know Sharon, you should be proud of yourself. You were confident in your solution and it's turned out to be good for everyone—all the way around."

"Thank you," Sharon said, with humility in her voice.

"And you?" Joan asked. "How are things going for you in the midst of all of this change?"

"I'm good. Just busy. Very busy in fact," Sharon explained. "We've got a week to prepare for a meeting we'll be having with the sales reps to explain the reorganization and new direction of the company. Things may be a little rocky here for a while."

"Major transitions will do that," Joan agreed. "Big changes can be traumatic, whether it's a divorce, a move to a different city, switching careers, or whatever. People's emotions tend to get a little ragged, so I hope you'll remember to tread lightly."

"Management seems to understand the difficulties."

"Sharon, it's not just management's job—but *everyone's*—to make sure things run smoothly. I think if you've learned anything out of all you've experienced in the past few months, it's that leadership can take place at any level. Since you started all these changes, lots of people, both above and below, are going to be watching to see how you make the transition."

"Thanks for the reminder, Joan."

"My pleasure. I just know how stressful transitions can be. I've had a few major ones in my own life, as I'm sure you have. The ones I handled best were the ones where someone was literally or figuratively holding my hand and telling me what was happening."

Sharon returned to work with a new commitment to try and make things flow more smoothly. She was amused at the rumors running wildly through SSI in the days preceding the meeting. She had reps asking her if she was being fired, if they were being fired, if SSI had been sold, or if SSI was replacing its sales force with phone staff as had happened at Reese. It amazed her how fast some people wanted to make things up to fill in their gaps in knowledge of what was really going on.

Sharon rehearsed a shorthand answer to the questions she got in the halls and in the elevator. She wanted to be reassuring, but did not want to get trapped into answering a thousand questions individually, that she, Alan, and Estelle would be answering in detail for the group on Thursday. She boiled it down to: "No one is getting fired, in fact, there will be a chance for us all to make a lot more money. I look forward to helping explain all the details at the meeting."

*   *   *   *   *   *   *   *   *   *   *   *

At the first of the focus groups, Alan was careful to rebut all of the rumors that were circulating at SSI. He and Sharon had made a list of all the scuttlebutt they had heard and Alan's opening remarks were designed to address them all. Sharon had told Alan her practice of trying to anticipate the questions a customer may have and answering those up front so the client is not worrying about them instead of listening to what she was saying.

Next Alan assured them that no one who wanted to keep

their job would lose it. "I know by now you have all heard what happened at Reese," he said. "We have no intention of eliminating our fine sales staff in favor of internal sales. Quite the contrary. We value your time and expertise too much to want to waste them servicing accounts which do not require your attention. We will not even ask you to give up any accounts you choose to keep. However, once Sharon explains the way we would like you to look at your customers, we believe you will see the value of turning over accounts which are no longer profitable for you to visit, to our new express-order department."

Alan introduced Sharon and turned the floor over to her. "I became tired," she began. "I got tired of racing faster and faster, squeezing in more sales calls but making fewer sales, and decided something had to change. I needed to focus on the best opportunities.

"In other words- if you wanted to sell private jets, you *could* take out a national ad in *TV Guide*. Granted, a few of the people who read *TV Guide* might actually be able to afford their own plane. But, we're talking about a very small percentage. And, don't forget that an advertisement in *TV Guide* would be rather expensive—not to mention how time consuming it would be to follow those leads, most of which would be dead-ends.

"But, say you had a chance to meet with one person—say, Bill Gates. Fly him to Monaco on one of your jets, wine him and dine him. You're odds are much better than when you were targeting the entire nation. The reason being is that *you know Bill Gates can afford a jet.* That effort focused on a single customer who is likely to buy is better spent than trying to reach hundreds of thousands of people who are never going to be interested in what you are selling."

She explained how she had calculated her cost-per-sale and how few of her customers ever made that back. She turned the floor back over to Alan.

"You may remember Pareto's Law," he began, "that 20 percent of your customers give you 80 percent of your business. I think once you examine your customers, you'll see that your efforts, and SSI's money, could be better utilized going after the 20 percent and turning the other 80 percent over to inside sales."

He went on to explain the filtering system of dividing clients into three categories: A, B and C. Alan then handed out the analysis he had prepared for Estelle and asked for the reps' input. Alan explained that, in this new world of SSI which they would create, competitive advantage would come not from R & D as it used to, but at the customer interface: Salespeople becoming knowledgeable partners in their clients' businesses.

After a lengthy discussion period, during which they all voiced their opinions of the new plan—varying from skepticism to a complete acceptance—Alan told them to take their time to look things over and draw their own conclusions. If they agreed that it all made sense, he challenged them to pick one account of their choice to be their first corporate account, as Sharon had ToolTech. They would then have to begin to research that account thoroughly. It would be the one on which they would train in the new approach with the new software applications. In the meantime they would continue to sell 4.0 and 5.0 to clients which were not going to be either their corporate account or the ones turned over to inside sales.

There was a question and answer period when the presentations ended. Alan had arranged for refreshments and had Erick, Vicky, Syed, Estelle, and Sharon, as well as himself, mingling to answer individual questions from the salespeople.

The meeting seemed to go well, especially considering how little time they had to prepare. Alan had to do most of the prep since Sharon was still very busy working with Erick and ToolTech on the software. Both she and Alan agreed keeping the ToolTech deal on track, and moving along, still had to be her first priority. The easiest way to prove the new system to the reps would be to have this huge sale go through as planned.

* * * * * * * * * * * *

The day after the meeting, Sharon was waiting for the elevator and surprised to hear the familiar voice of her former co-worker. "Good morning, Sharon."

"Craig! What're you doing here?"

"I work here," he said casually.

"You do?"

"I will," he said, dropping the casual act and beaming. "Alan called me last evening. Said Keith stuck around after the meeting and wants to take him up on the early retirement deal. I guess I'll take over Keith's larger accounts and be the first official member of your new sales team."

"That's great!"

They rode up on the elevator together.

"It sounds like there'll be some great opportunities here again. It feels good to be back. There'll be a lot of work, but also the rewards and challenges my current job just can't offer. I'm going to see Alan and then head over to my job and give notice."

"Good to have you back. It'll be work, that's for sure. But worth it," Sharon agreed.

"Sounds exciting to me."

"It will be. I'll have to make one last call on my smaller accounts, to introduce them to whomever it is we hire to run the inside sales system, so they can explain how that works. We may lose a few clients, but for the most part, we want as smooth a transition as possible, all the way around. We're working on a transition plan to make sure all aspects of SSI— especially the people—can make this move with as little disruption as possible. We have to keep the salespeople happy,

157

and hopefully successful in selling the older versions, to maintain cash flow until we all learn this new consulting approach."

"And I guess, according to Alan, you are expecting some turnover with people who can't or won't want to change. Besides Keith?"

"Possibly. And I can't blame him for wanting out. It could take months to a year to get everything ready for an opportunity like ToolTech. He's only a couple years from retirement, and his health isn't all that great, I guess. He's pounded the pavement a long time. I can see how that would wear you down. Not much sense in committing himself to such a major change that may not pay off for a while."

"It's going to take a lot of research on these accounts. In the old days you could just kind of shoot from the hip as you went along, but this means really knowing your clients and every aspect of their businesses."

"I was never much for 'shooting from the hip,' but I know what you mean. There can be no bluffing when you're talking about being this in-depth with such a narrow focus," Sharon added.

On The Green

**Are you able to effectively manage
the new strategy inside your organization?**

- Do you have a "change management strategy" for your initiative?
- Have the key individuals "bought in" to the message?

New corporate initiatives often fail because the people responsible for operationalizing the new behavior and role changes don't "buy in" to the strategy. As a result, people will spend their energies in a defensive mode. They try to protect themselves, and, as a result, sales/corporate performance takes a plunge.

It is necessary for senior management to lead these change initiatives and make sure that the employees have "bought in" and are committed. If not, employees often feel like victims and will consciously or unconsciously sabotage the initiative. Leadership needs to treat this change process the same way salespeople must treat customers:

- Trust needs to be established.
- A participative-needs analysis must be created.
- Using a creative process, solutions need to be identified.
- The tools and support needed to help people and the organization go through the necessary learning curves needs to be provided.

Without employing this process, most change initiatives are destined for failure.

These changes require an effective transition plan from their leaders. These leaders need to understand that you have to be hard and clear on the business problem, but "soft on the people" process. Soft on the people doesn't mean that people are allowed to forget performance requirements. It does require an understanding that, for people to embrace change, they have to be supported through "endings".

Endings are emotionally rooted in past successes and require a listening strategy. If "endings" are dealt with effectively, people can move through transitions smoothly so that they can embrace "new beginnings".

For organizations to grow, people have to grow. Leadership is no longer only a senior executive role in today's rapidly changing environment: Leadership is a requirement at all levels of an organization. Sharon and Jeff rise to the occasion of becoming key leaders in their organizations.

CHAPTER ELEVEN

In the cup

ToolTech Vice President Bill Atkinson, along with Lorenzo Ortiz, Jeff Lee, and Sharon Kelly sat on the plush sofas of Jon Gregory's palatial office. A large aquarium lined half of one wall, next to display cases. Two full walls of glass offered a commanding view of San Diego. His desk, Sharon thought, was large enough to double as a helipad. After Gregory's secretary had served them coffee, Atkinson quickly opened his briefcase and buried his head in work. Sharon and Jeff sat nervously waiting and drinking their coffee, while Lorenzo got up and began to pace the office.

As he scanned the shelves looking at books and knick-knacks, his eyes stopped on a golf club in a glass case. He turned to Jeff and Sharon. "Check this out. The plaque says it's Bobby Jones' putter."

"It is," a voice coming through the door answered.

They all turned to face Jon Gregory, the president of ToolTech.

Gregory walked over to Lorenzo, carefully opened the glass case, took out the putter, and with the gentle hands of a father lifting his newborn child for the first time, handed the putter to Lorenzo.

"I bought it at an auction about eight years ago. I'm sure I paid way too much for it, but I had to have it."

Lorenzo nodded appreciatively as he reverently examined the club.

"Do you play?"

"Yes," Ortiz answered. "So do Sharon and Jeff. In fact, she has us recruited for a charity golf outing at Mountain View Country Club."

"Mountain View?" Gregory smiled. "I haven't played

there in years. Great course. My only hole-in-one was on their sixth hole. An uphill par 3. Used a 4-iron, with the wind at my back. Wind blew it in. Dumb luck."

"Nice. Never had a hole-in-one myself."

"You've got a few more years of play in you; it could happen. I belong to Willow Wood, but I hardly have time to play anymore. Need to get back to it. And to Mountain View."

Sharon and Jeff had walked over to join Lorenzo and Gregory in front of the glass case. Lorenzo, Sharon, and Jeff carefully passed around the putter so as to still have a hand free to shake Gregory's.

As she shook Gregory's hand, Sharon said, "I hope this isn't presumptuous, but given that you play and are anxious to play Mountain View again…. The three of us are playing in that charity thing a week from Saturday, if you would care to join us?"

Ortiz nodded. "It's a shotgun event. We could use a fourth."

"I begged off," Atkinson said.

"I know, Bill," Gregory joked, "you've often expressed your disdain for the game. Are you still taking those ridiculously long bicycle rides?"

"Every weekend."

"Well, you'll see the light and join the rest of the world on the links one of these days."

Atkinson shook his head. "Thanks, Jon, but I'll leave that game to you." He declined Jeff's offer of the putter, so Jeff handed it back to Gregory who returned it to its case.

"I realize Jones was a bit before your time. He was before mine, too, but I still think he was the greatest golfer ever. Have you heard of him?"

"Of course," Sharon answered.

The door to the office swung open and Gregory's secretary, who ushered Sharon and the others in minutes early now admitted Michael Carlson, Alan Miller, Estelle Washington, and SSI's corporate legal counsel. They had no sooner arrived than the secretary let in another wave consisting of the rest of the ToolTech contingent: their lawyer; CFO; MIS director, Alex Knust; and the VP of marketing.

"Nice to finally meet you after all this talking on the phone," was the comment most commonly heard as the groups exchanged pleasantries.

Jon Gregory led the way into a conference room adjacent to his office. The conference room, like the sitting room area, had an eagle's eye view of San Diego—looking across the harbor at the Navy base and the Coronado Bridge. The large table was of fine, inlaid wood in keeping with all of the other royal appointments. Sharon could not help wondering if the furniture in this room cost more than all of the furniture in her house. Maybe more than the house itself. Each place at the table had been set with a neat stack of documents and folders along with a name card beckoning each of the participants to their assigned place.

The group grew silent as everyone took their seats, except Michael Carlson, SSI's president. He looked to his counterpart from ToolTech as though for permission, and Jon Gregory nodded approval.

"Mr. Gregory, I have spoken to you so often on the phone," Carlson began, "and, Mr. Ortiz and Mr. Atkinson, I've heard so much about you both and all of your hard work on this project, that I feel as though I already know each of you. Jeff Lee, on the other hand, I actually do know. It seems like he's always at SSI. I often ask him if doesn't have an office of his own to go home to," Carlson joked.

"He does, but Sharon is always in it," Ortiz kidded back.

The group chuckled.

"Actually, it is great how well our people get along." Carlson smiled. "They've been putting forth a lot of effort, and there is much more to be done, but I am confident with the skilled input from the key individuals at ToolTech that we will be able to deliver the cost-savings outlined in this agreement." Carlson held up his copy as proof. "It will be on schedule and it'll be right."

He smiled at Sharon as he said this. She nodded and smiled back. In their last strategy session before this signing ceremony, Sharon had emphasized to Mr. Carlson how important it was that he reaffirm to the assembled hierarchy of ToolTech just how solidly all of SSI was behind this business solution. Her close working relationship with Jeff had made it possible for her to keep abreast of the rumors inside ToolTech and she wanted to deal with them appropriately. She had heard grumbles, particularly from the head of ToolTech's information systems, Alex Knust, that there was some doubt that SSI, which had been selling off-the-shelf software with just minor variations, was capable of delivering a huge software package which would interface so many different key business processes across so many different departments.

Carlson assured Sharon he would only be too happy to make it clear that he was willing to commit whichever of SSI's resources were necessary to make this project successful. He had asked for her help in preparing his speech to make sure he covered all of the points. Sharon was impressed that although it was the speech they had written, he was not reading it; it was as if he were speaking extemporaneously rather than making canned remarks.

He understood as well as she did that if SSI dropped the ball on this one that the chance of getting another shot at ToolTech's business for years to come, or having any other company trust them with a software overhaul, was nil.

Carlson went on, "My office and my staff are available to provide whatever service and help necessary to bring every ToolTech department on-line as quickly as possible."

Sharon decided she liked Carlson's inclusive style, the way he made eye contact and smiled at each person in the room, the way he not only remembered names, but job titles, functions, and what each person had actually contributed to this deal. She had noted he was like this at SSI where he remembered every employee he had ever met.

He continued his speech without ever making it sound like a sales pitch or that he was running for office. By the time he sat down, the tension Sharon had initially felt among the participants of this summit meeting was gone.

Jon Gregory took the floor and first thanked Carlson, Sharon, and the rest of the SSI team before saying, "Of course it took the board's approval to spend this amount of money and make these kinds of changes in the way we do business. Coming on the heels of the CTC acquisition, there were questions about the cost and necessity of making such major changes, but when Sharon was able to quantify for the board the long-term cost savings and the overall benefits such a restructuring could provide, they voted unanimously to support it. I invited you all here today to officially sign the contracts that promise to give ToolTech a competitive edge and I hope will be the start of a relationship which will lead ToolTech to a new level of growth and efficiency."

    *   *   *   *   *   *   *   *   *   *   *   *

Sharon assembled her foursome near the parking lot before leading them off to find Joan. As they carried their clubs toward the check-in tent, Jon Gregory said, "Excuse me, but I see an old friend I have to say hello to." Then he called out, "Mrs. Moore!"

The woman stopped and turned. "Mr. Gregory, what a nice surprise!"

Sharon was shocked to see who had answered Gregory's call. "Joan!"

"Sharon!" Joan came trotting over. She gave Sharon half a hug as she shook Gregory's hand.

"You two know each other?" All three said at once, then

laughed that they had all spoken in unison. They all tried to speak again at once, then all stopped.

"Somebody say something," Joan said.

"You just did," Sharon laughed.

'Well, since I'm the oldest and it's my tournament, I get to decide who talks first. Sharon."

Sharon asked Joan and Gregory, "How do you two know each other?"

"I've known Mr. Gregory forever, it seems."

Gregory added, "Mrs. Moore is on the board of ToolTech. Chairperson emeritus—"

"That means I only go to the meetings I want to," she joked, interrupting. "And organizing this little golf outing has kept me from attending for a while."

Gregory continued, "I know. We miss you," he said to Joan before turning back to Sharon. "Mrs. Moore's father founded the company, but in the forty years that she ran it, she built it from a little 'mom and pop,' into the multinational it is. I had no idea it was her tournament you were dragging me to. I might have known she was chairing another good cause!"

Joan looked at Sharon suddenly realizing what Gregory's presence meant. "You mean to tell me ToolTech was the company you kept telling me about?" She turned to Jeff. "Every time you mentioned *Jeff's company*, you meant ToolTech?"

"Hello, Joan. Good to see you again," Jeff nodded as they shook hands.

Sharon laughed. "I can't believe that all the time you were giving me advice, that it was about your own company!"

"I just hope it was good advice. I still own a lot of stock."

"It was brilliant advice," Sharon reassured her.

"I can't believe that your foursome includes one of my oldest associates," Joan marveled. "I hired Jon as a sales rep in nineteen—"

"Isn't it about tee time?" Gregory interrupted. "And no sense aging either one of us more than we have to." They all

166

laughed. "ToolTech still believes in promotion from within. Today we brought a couple of our rising stars. I believe you've met Jeff, and this is Lorenzo Ortiz, our head of transportation."

"Joan Moore," she smiled, as she extended her hand.

In The Cup

The ToolTech opportunity has tremendous potential for leverage at SSI. The intellectual capital that will be gained by SSI as they create the *Enterprise 2.0* for ToolTech will create leading-edge technology for their brand products. These brand products will be sold at higher margins throughout all of SSI's distribution channels and account for rapid growth and profitability.

The major source of intellectual capital in the future will come from the sales interface—capturing Sharon's experience—with an organization that listens.

CHAPTER TWELVE

Turning pro

As Sharon rode the elevator to the top floor of Software Solutions Inc.'s low-rise building, she thought about how much life had changed in the past few months. She now knew almost every inch of this building from the engineering department in the basement through marketing on the second floor, past sales on the next floor, distribution on the fourth, on up, to the office of the president which sat in one corner of the uppermost floor.

The first time she had received a phone call similar to the one she just got, it had scared her. The voice on the other end of the phone line said simply, "Ms. Kelly? Michael Carlson here. I was wondering if it would be too much trouble for you to come up to my office at some point. At your convenience, of course."

Although the tone had been friendly, that call six months ago had terrified her. She had dropped what she was doing and hurried the length of the building to the elevators, but when one did not come immediately, she took the stairs two flights up to Mr. Carlson's office. The first such summons made her feel like she was being called to the principal's office and the jog up the stairs had helped her to calm her nerves and burn off some of the butterflies.

Those fears seemed silly now. Michael Carlson's friendly manner was as it always had been. She was now almost as familiar with his office as she was with her own. His office was as down-to-earth as his personality. None of the trappings of power like the high-tower office of Jon Gregory, the president of ToolTech. Carlson's office was not furnished much better than her own office, and not even as well as Estelle Washington's. As she got off the elevator on his floor, she could not believe Carlson had ever intimidated her so much. They were now working together on such a regular basis that it no longer seemed odd that she was once again on her way to the executive suite, such as it was.

She was surprised to be shown into the president's office while he was still on the phone. Carlson motioned for her to take a seat.

"Hang on, Jon," he said into the mouthpiece. Looking at Sharon he said, "I have Jon Gregory from ToolTech on the phone. He wants to set up a golf game with you."

Sharon hoped she did not sound too startled when she said, "Really?"

Carlson pressed a button on the phone and hung up the handset. "You still there, Jon?" he asked into a speaker.

"Still here."

"I'm always afraid I'll lose people doing that."

"I'm not lost."

"Good."

"Sharon?" the disembodied voice asked.

"Yes, Mr. Gregory?"

"I was telling my friend, Ray Williams," Sharon knew the name sounded familiar, but before she could place it, Jon Gregory went on, "of Surway, about the package you put together for us."

Sharon had seen the name of the president of the pharmaceutical giant, Surway, in enough business publications, but out of context she did not make the connection immediately.

"And he'd like to hear more about it. I suggested a golf game if you're interested."

With Carlson watching her, she did not want to follow her first impulse and leap out of her chair and start dancing around the room. She was tempted to at least high-five the president whose eyes had also widened at the prospect of selling software to a mega-corp like Surway. She forced herself to calmly answer, "Of course."

There was a time when meeting with a company president would have caused her to lose sleep from now until the day of the golf match. Now she traveled in and out of the president's office with a freedom and confidence that a year ago she would not have been sure she possessed. She still technically reported to Alan, but was almost as likely to be meeting with Michael Carlson as with her immediate boss. Her deals no longer belonged just to the sales department, but touched every corner of SSI.

Over at ToolTech, Jeff Lee was feeling the same sense of freedom, floating to all parts of the company. He said he felt at times like an 'ambassador without a portfolio,' having the power and authority to function wherever and however he had to.

"I know you won't be able to give him specifics on the golf course, but thought you could outline a few general things."

"Certainly."

"How is Friday at two?"

"I don't have my calendar in front of me, but I think that works. I'll check it as soon as I get back down to my office and call you if there is a change."

"Okay. Are you up for it Michael?"

"Hang on a second, would you Jon?"

"Sure."

Carlson hit a button on the phone and looked at Sharon. "I know this could be a big deal for us, but do you need me there?"

"It would be great to have you along, sir."

"It's Michael, not 'sir,' or 'Mr. Carlson,' remember?" He said with a smile.

"Sorry. Force of habit. Michael."

"And the question was, do you *need* me there?"

Sharon's brow furrowed. So her boss explained, "My son has a violin recital at school on Friday, and I would really like to go, but if you think this is vital...."

Sharon nodded understandingly. "I think for a meeting as preliminary as this, I can handle it."

"Oh, I *know* you can handle it. But I just didn't know if you wanted me to lend the weight of my office to this."

"Not really necessary. Might actually intimidate Mr. Williams if we bring out our big guns right away."

"Good. I really don't like golf anyway," he smiled. "Let me know when you need me to jump in on this one." He pressed the phone button again. "Jon?"

"Still here."

"Good. I was just checking. I have a prior commitment on Friday. Did you really want me along? I could see what I might be able to do...."

"Honestly, it's Sharon he wants to meet. And I've seen you play golf," Gregory laughed.

"Nice to know I'm wanted," Carlson laughed back.

"Sharon, got any ideas for a fourth?"

"Since Joan just got me to join Mountain View how about if we play there and ask her to join us?"

"Excellent idea. And you know I love that course."

"Shall I call her?"

After they wrapped up the phone call, Carlson clicked off the phone. "You joined Mountain View?" he asked, impressed.

"Yes."

"You have to know someone to get in there," he smiled, teasing.

"Joan. Mrs. Moore. She's been very good to me. We've been playing golf together about once a week for months now. So, when she asked me to join Mountain View, I couldn't say *no*."

He nodded. "Mountain View should impress Ray Williams. I've never met him. Just seen him at a few functions. I get the impression he's not an easy man to impress."

"I'll have to do a little research, so I make sure that I handle him just right, then. And I know nothing about pharmaceuticals, so I'll have a lot to learn on that topic as well."

"I know you'll be thorough. Besides the golf game, there was something else I wanted to see you about—and just finished talking to Jon Gregory about—when you got here." He handed her a folder. "The first half-year report on ToolTech."

Sharon's eyes widened. She started to open the folder.

"The numbers are nowhere close to what we projected."

Sharon looked up like a deer in the headlights.

"Okay, bad joke. Sorry," Carlson said. "They are way over what we projected. How could you doubt that? Did you see what kind of a bonus they gave Jon Gregory at the close of their fiscal year? Their stock was looking so good, I bought some and I never play the market."

"I bought some, too. Not only was it a good investment— it's almost tripled since I bought it—it gives me a little extra incentive to do a good job with them."

"Between their buying CTC and the job we—or I should say *you*—have done in streamlining their operations, they ought to give *you* a bonus!"

"Thanks, Michael."

"And we will be giving you a bonus at the end of the year. Estelle and I haven't worked out all the details of how and how much, but you sure have changed the way this company does business. Or, I should say, even *looks* at business."

Sharon was stunned to think that on top of the huge commission checks she had been getting she would be getting a bonus, too. It was hard to believe that last year at this time, she was getting behind on her mortgage and worried about keeping her job.

Times *had* changed. For the better.

GOING

FOR THE

GREEN

SELLING IN THE
21ST CENTURY

Appendixes

Appendix A

Tables of Organization

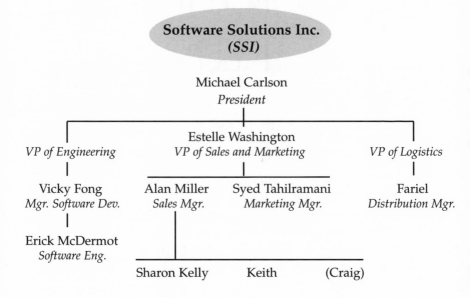

**Software Solutions Inc.
(SSI)**

Michael Carlson
President

VP of Engineering

Estelle Washington
VP of Sales and Marketing

VP of Logistics

Vicky Fong
Mgr. Software Dev.

Alan Miller
Sales Mgr.

Syed Tahilramani
Marketing Mgr.

Fariel
Distribution Mgr.

Erick McDermot
Software Eng.

Sharon Kelly   Keith   (Craig)

SSI's main competitors:

LatCo; Monica Matthews is their rep.

Reese—Has had to give up its sales force due to decrease in sales.

E.F. Striepeke is one of Sharon's minor clients.

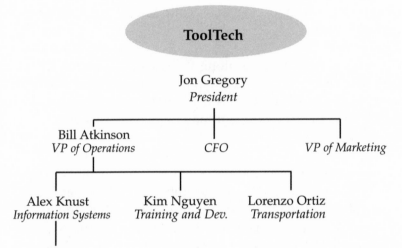

ToolTech

Jon Gregory
President

Bill Atkinson
VP of Operations

CFO

VP of Marketing

Alex Knust
Information Systems

Kim Nguyen
Training and Dev.

Lorenzo Ortiz
Transportation

Ann
Purchasing Director

Jeff Lee
Software Buyer

ToolTech is about to merge with
California Tool Company (CTC), to become
the largest tool company in their field.

Appendix B

Golf Terms

Most golf courses are comprised of 18 holes. The first nine are called the "front 9," and the second half of the course is called the "back 9."

Most courses have hazards along the way—trees, bunkers (also called sand traps), and small bodies of water to make play more challenging. Golf is usually played by groups of four players (a **Foursome**), but may be played by fewer players in a group.

Different, specialized clubs are used for different shots. The common names for some of these clubs are: the **Driver** (used for long shots off the tee); **Woods** (numbered 1 through 5), also used for longer shots, either from the tee or fairway; **Irons** (numbered 1 through 9); **Wedges** (for shorter, higher shots, including a sand wedge for getting out of sand traps); and, a **Putter** (for a flat rolling stroke on the green).

Par - The number of strokes a reasonably competent golfer could be expected to make on a hole, or for the course. Most holes are par 3, 4 or 5, and par for a standard course is 72. It is assumed that a golfer, to make par on a par 4 hole, would take 2 strokes to get to the green, and then 2-putt on the green.

Bogey - One stroke more than par for a hole.

Double Bogey - Two over par for a hole.

Birdie - One under par.

A hole in one - A rare event of having the ball go into the hole on the first shot off the tee.

Mulligan - In a friendly game of golf, the courtesy of letting a player re-play a badly hit shot. Usually on a drive off the tee.

Best Ball - A type of tournament in which all members of the same team may play their shot from the spot where the "best ball" or best shot of any of them landed. This speeds up play, and allows for lower scores than play among casual players would usually generate. **Shotgun** tournaments start players on each of the eighteen holes simultaneously to speed up play.

Tee - The area from which a **Drive**, or long first shot, is made on any given hole; also the small wooden or plastic peg on which the ball is placed for such a shot. On most courses you can tee from one of several different areas, marked by colors. The **blue** or **gold tees** are for very good amateur players or professionals. The **white tees** are the ones most commonly used. The **red tees**, sometimes referred to as the "women's tees," are the ones closest to the hole. Since usually the only difference between a male and female golfer is his strength in hitting a longer drive, this shorter distance for a woman makes it possible for people of different sexes, but like abilities, to play as equals.

Gimme - A putt that is so short that it is assumed that the player would make it, so he or she does not even have to putt it in; as in "Give me."

Putt - A short, golf stroke played on the green. The **Green** is the very short grass that surrounds the hole. A **Lag** putt is a long putt deliberately left short so as to not overshoot the hole, but that makes the next putt an easy short one.

Bunker - A pit of sand that forms a hazard, or obstacle on the course. Once a ball lands in one of these "sand traps," it can be difficult to hit it out.

Honors - The "honor" to hit the first drive. The person who scored lowest (best) on the previous hole gets to tee off first. After that, on each hole, the player who is **"away**," that is, farthest from the hole gets to hit next, so players do not just take turns. This makes it easier for all of the players to be on the green at the same time. **Up** refers to being "up" on the green, in a position to just putt it in. Once everyone is up, they all putt.

Rough - The long grass and weeds that border a fairway.

Fairway - The nicely kept part of the hole, leading from the tee to the green.

Flag - The numbered pendant that marks each hole or "the pin."

Clubhouse - The building on a golf course usually containing a bar, restaurant, restrooms, pro shop, etc.

LPGA - The Ladies Professional Golf Association.

Appendix C

About the Author

**Douglas K. Peterson,
consultant, author, speaker, and facilitator.**

President of Leadership Technologies, Inc., one of the leading
agencies in the Wilson Learning network, Doug Peterson has
more than 26 years of experience in the consulting, facilitating, and training arenas. Peterson entered the field in 1971 as
managing director of Advanced Business Management
(ABM), a San Rafael, California, training and consulting firm.
In an 18-month period, he took the company from $.3 million
in sales to $5 million.

In 1972, he became managing director of ABM International,
establishing business operations in Europe, Asia, and Africa.

Peterson then moved to Switzerland in 1974 when he became
senior partner of Ravice International, a firm specializing in
test marketing products, license agreements and distribution
agreements with major international firms.

During the years of 1976 to 1982, Peterson established himself
with Wilson Learning. He became owner of the Wilson
Learning agency in South Africa, providing consulting and
training services to major international clients including:
Liberty Life, Old Mutual Insurance Company, Standard Bank,
Barclay's Bank, BMW, Toyota, Volkswagon, IBM, and
Computer Sciences Corporation.

In 1983, Peterson returned to the United States as the north-
east regional vice president of Wilson Learning. He was
responsible for such national accounts as IBM, AT&T, New

York Life, Citibank, Amerada Hess, and Chemical Bank.

Two years later, in 1985, Peterson became the owner and principal of Leadership Technologies, Inc., an authorized Wilson Learning agency. Based in Los Angeles, Leadership Technologies has four offices: two are located in the Southern California areas of Long Beach and San Diego; the others are in Johnson City, Tennessee and Minneapolis, Minnesota. The agency's client base, however, extends throughout the United States and Canada. The agency's core competency rests with helping companies firmly establish their sales force as a source of strategic advantage.

In 1995, Peterson was selected to become part of the Global Solutions Group, a separate division within Wilson Learning. Global Solutions focuses on worldwide opportunities, emerging technologies and senior level relationships with Fortune 500 global companies.

Sharon nodded understandingly. "I think for a meeting as preliminary as this, I can handle it."

"Oh, I *know* you can handle it. But I just didn't know if you wanted me to lend the weight of my office to this."

"Not really necessary. Might actually intimidate Mr. Williams if we bring out our big guns right away."

"Good. I really don't like golf anyway," he smiled. "Let me know when you need me to jump in on this one." He pressed the phone button again. "Jon?"

"Still here."

"Good. I was just checking. I have a prior commitment on Friday. Did you really want me along? I could see what I might be able to do...."

"Honestly, it's Sharon he wants to meet. And I've seen you play golf," Gregory laughed.

"Nice to know I'm wanted," Carlson laughed back.

"Sharon, got any ideas for a fourth?"

"Since Joan just got me to join Mountain View how about if we play there and ask her to join us?"

"Excellent idea. And you know I love that course."

"Shall I call her?"

After they wrapped up the phone call, Carlson clicked off the phone. "You joined Mountain View?" he asked, impressed.

"Yes."

"You have to know someone to get in there," he smiled, teasing.

"Joan. Mrs. Moore. She's been very good to me. We've been playing golf together about once a week for months now. So, when she asked me to join Mountain View, I couldn't say *no*."

He nodded. "Mountain View should impress Ray Williams. I've never met him. Just seen him at a few functions. I get the impression he's not an easy man to impress."

"I'll have to do a little research, so I make sure that I handle him just right, then. And I know nothing about pharmaceuti-

There was a time when meeting with a company president would have caused her to lose sleep from now until the day of the golf match. Now she traveled in and out of the president's office with a freedom and confidence that a year ago she would not have been sure she possessed. She still technically reported to Alan, but was almost as likely to be meeting with Michael Carlson as with her immediate boss. Her deals no longer belonged just to the sales department, but touched every corner of SSI.

Over at ToolTech, Jeff Lee was feeling the same sense of freedom, floating to all parts of the company. He said he felt at times like an 'ambassador without a portfolio,' having the power and authority to function wherever and however he had to.

"I know you won't be able to give him specifics on the golf course, but thought you could outline a few general things."

"Certainly."

"How is Friday at two?"

"I don't have my calendar in front of me, but I think that works. I'll check it as soon as I get back down to my office and call you if there is a change."

"Okay. Are you up for it Michael?"

"Hang on a second, would you Jon?"

"Sure."

Carlson hit a button on the phone and looked at Sharon. "I know this could be a big deal for us, but do you need me there?"

"It would be great to have you along, sir."

"It's Michael, not 'sir,' or 'Mr. Carlson,' remember?" He said with a smile.

"Sorry. Force of habit. Michael."

"And the question was, do you *need* me there?"

Sharon's brow furrowed. So her boss explained, "My son has a violin recital at school on Friday, and I would really like to go, but if you think this is vital...."

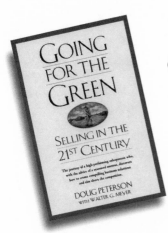

Order Another Copy Today!

GOING FOR THE GREEN

SELLING IN THE 21ST CENTURY

BY: DOUG PETERSON

NAME_____

ADDRESS_____

CITY_____

STATE_____ZIP_____

PHONE_____

E-MAIL_____

PRICES: 1-10 books, $24.95 each
10-50 books, $22.95 each
50-100 books, $19.95 each
*(Please call for price
breaks on large orders)*

SHIPPING: Add $4.00 for one book, plus
$2.00 for each additional book.

QUANTITY_____TOTAL $_____
(Tennessee Residents must add 8.5% Sales Tax)

PAYMENT:
❑ Check   ❑ Credit Card
    ❑ American Express   ❑ Visa
    ❑ MasterCard   ❑ Discover

CARD NUMBER_____

NAME ON CARD_____

EXP. DATE_____

Please mail this form to:
LTI Publishing
116 Lands End Court, Suite 100
Piney Flats, TN 37686

Phone, Fax, or Web orders to:
(877)244-5664
Fax (423)283-9302
ltipublishing.com
going4thegreen.com